I0642006

The Natural Man

The
Natural Man

HENRY DAVID THOREAU

compiled by
Robert Epstein and Sherry Phillips

This publication made possible
with the assistance of the Kern Foundation.

The Theosophical Publishing House

Wheaton, IL • Madras, India • London, England

Original Quest Book edition, 1978, published by the
Theosophical Publishing House, a department of the
Theosophical Society in America. Third printing 1988

Library of Congress Cataloging in Publication Data.

Thoreau. Henry David, 1817—1862
  The natural man.

  (A Quest book)
  Bibliography: p.
  1. Thoreau, Henry David, 1817—1862—Quotations.
I. Epstein, Robert. II. Phillips, Sherry. III. Title.
PS3042.E6   1978   818'.3'09   77-18122
ISBN 0-8356-0503-5 pbk.

Printed in the United States of America

To my Grandparents
and Godparents
and the memory of
Morris Deutsch and Louis Salamon

In memory of
my Grandmother,
Rebecca Wasserman

—The Editors
R. E. and S. P.

As I have said, I do not propose to write an ode to dejection, but to brag as lustily as chanticleer in the morning, standing on his roost, if only to wake my neighbors up.

Walden, "Where I Lived and What I Lived For"

CONTENTS

Foreword ix

WHO I AM 1

MAN 5

   Self-Realization 6
   Men and Women 9
   Society 11
   Friendship 15
   Solitude 16
   Love 18
   Marriage 20
   Chastity 21
   Bravery 22
   My Contemporaries 22

LIFE 29

   Simplicity 31
   Money 32
   Business and Labor 34
   True Wealth . . . , ... 36
   Possessions 38
   Gifts 40
   Health 41
   Food 43
   The Senses 47
   Dreams 48
   Death 48

NATURE 50

   Natural Phenomenon 54
   Oceans, Rivers and Lakes 56
   Walden Pond 58
   Trees 59
   Flowers, Weeds, and Fruits 60
   Animals 63
   Birds 65
   Time 66
   Seasons 69
   Sounds and Silence 71
   Beauty 73
   Colors 73
   Walking 75
   The Indian 76

KNOWLEDGE AND IGNORANCE 79

   Facts 80
   Wisdom 81
   Thought 82
   Conscience 83
   Philosophy 83
   Genius 84
   Education 85
   History 87

ART 89

   Music 90
   Poetry 91
   The Poet 92

The Writer 94
Reading 95
Writing 96
Journal 99
Books 101

RELIGION 102
God 104
Scriptures 106
Spiritual Purity 108
Virtue 109
Truth 110
Sincerity 112
Philanthropy 112
Humanitarianism 113

Bibliography 115

Suggested Reading 118

FOREWORD

Who was Henry David Thoreau? Judged by his fame today, he was a writer: *Walden,* the second of Thoreau's books published in his lifetime, is universally acclaimed as one of the major contributions to modern literature. *"Civil Disobedience"* is likewise considered the classic statement of passive resistance, the essay serving as the inspiration to Gandhi's nonviolent movement in India. And the massive *Journal,* the primary source for such works as *The Maine Woods, A Yankee in Canada,* and *A Week on the Concord and Merrimack Rivers,* is regarded by many as Thoreau's crowning achievement, the culmination of his life's work.

Though his writing reflected his genius, Thoreau's literary accomplishments serve as a mirror for the inner man who was Thoreau; for he embodied, in his own life, an ethical and spiritual ideal toward which many before and still others after him have aspired. He was not content simply to espouse lofty goals and ideas: he fulfilled them and defended them. Above all, Henry Thoreau stood among his peers as a man of principle, of uncompromising ethical integrity. Emerson best captured the essence of Thoreau's greatness when he declared in the funeral address he delivered upon the death of his friend: "Thoreau was sincerity itself, and might fortify the convictions of prophets in the ethical laws by his holy living." Thoreau, in short, had dedicated his life to "the art of living well."

Not merely a lover of nature, Thoreau was an astute naturalist. He roamed the hills and forests in and around Concord, attending to the wonders of the countryside with a poet's sensitivity and a scientist's eye. But this outdoorsman strikes one as no ordinary observer of nature; while recognizing the vast knowledge to be gained by close and sedulous study of the environment, Thoreau apprehended the impenetrable mystery in which the universe is shrouded. His study of nature was characterized first and foremost by reverence and awe and not by a thirst for conquest and control. He worshipped the environment and lamented its gradual destruction by industrial expansion and the concomitant pollution of natural resources. No mere sentimentalist, Thoreau foresaw, and warned against, the ecological poverty of which our age despairs. He intuited in his lifetime what it has taken others more than a century to learn: that man cannot continue to ravage and exploit nature with impunity. He cannot continue to bulldoze the landscape and pave it over with asphalt and concrete, for without "the tonic of wildness" the environment soon becomes a barren wasteland. "In Wildness" Thoreau eloquently proclaimed, "is the preservation of the World."

Similarly, in the world of human affairs, Thoreau denounced the stale and stultifying conventions which fostered conformity at the expense of individual self-exploration. He was an inveterate foe of tradition-for-tradition's sake, substituting instead the ever-flowing medium of self-inquiry. No institution stood unchallenged by Thoreau in his lifelong pursuit after truth; he deplored hypocrisy, ignorance, and injustice in any form. Some men compromise, others surrender to the prejudices of their time; Thoreau denounced inequity whether in church or state or society. Slavery outraged him and he not only spoke out loudly against it but effectually acted out his part in abolishing it. Thoreau's imprisonment for refusing to pay the tax supporting slavery is recounted in his essay "On the Duty of Civil Disobedience."

For the author of *Walden,* spirituality was more than perfunctory devotion to performing sacraments and reciting prayers: the truly religious express their faith in their Creator by reverencing nature and nurturing humanity. "Our religion," Thoreau reminded his neighbors, "is where our love is."

The ethical dimension to Thoreau's life has not been fully appreciated. He valued honesty, truth, and sincerity in human relations, and practiced a rigorous self-discipline in every aspect of life. Although Thoreau never married, his remarks on love, chastity, and sensuality bear the mark of intense self-reflection. In dietary matters he counselled moderation and self-control. Thoreau in actual life rarely, if ever, ate meat and renounced hunting whether for food or sport, convinced that carnivorous living was contrary to all that is divine in man's being. His chapter on "Higher Laws" in *Walden,* the most complete statement of the New Englander's moral convictions, includes a powerful defense of vegetarianism. It is, in fact, one of the classic contributions to the literature of the meatless movement, having influenced countless numbers of vegetarians and humanitarians who have chosen to live more simply, innocently, and in harmony with nature.

He preached and practiced a doctrine of simplicity against the expanding industrialization of his generation. The cabin he built for himself at Walden Pond, the bean patch he cultivated and maintained, and his rambles in the woods, were all expressions of the simple mode of living he embraced. Thoreau believed that most men were employed in vain pursuits, that the true labor of man was to be found in nature and not in factories, and so encouraged all to seek their salvation out-of-doors.

This sage advice the New Englander directed especially toward young intellectuals who were accustomed to being told that scholars require the quiet sanctuary of the library for their studies. Not so for Thoreau, himself a graduate of Harvard College. He shovelled manure, labored in the fields, and surveyed swamp lands when he was not walking through the woods; and he exhorted those in college to find similar gainful employments.

Thoreau, in fact, did not place a special value on conventional knowledge, that cramping accumulation of facts taught by our educational institutions. True knowledge one cannot learn in the schools. To learn anything at all of enduring worth, one needs the freedom and flexibility which no institution—however liberal it may be—can provide. Education, for Thoreau, meant self-realization; a process by which the individual unfolds new layers of awareness through contact with his real self, what Thoreau called ''the perennial source of our life.''

The highest order of intelligence attainable by human

beings, therefore, is that of the poet and philosopher, insofar as both retain the ineffable pleasure for life which children intuitively possess. In the ecstasy of living—in being fully and consciously awake—Thoreau found the wisdom of the ages. The poet's language is the language of this spirit and its translation is the task of the philosopher. Understood in these terms, Thoreau believed that the best poetry is always mythological, while philosophy evolves into scripture. The writing of *Walden,* indeed, was the creation of a fable—epitomized by the two parables in the ''Conclusion'' to the book—and couched in the spiritual framework of the author's deepest religious experience. It is this view of writing as sacred mythology which accounts for the poetic quality of Thoreau's finest prose for, though he may not have possessed the technical skill of the bard, he had, as Emerson succinctly put it, ''the source of poetry in his spiritual perception.''

Through the senses union with the divine is achieved, Thoreau avowed. At the highest level of consciousness where every faculty is alive the individual merges with the sights, sounds, and smells of nature in a moment of perfect harmony that culminates in enlightenment. Thoreau describes his enlightenment experience in ''Sounds'' from *Walden:*

Sometimes, in a summer morning, having taken my accustomed bath, I sat in my sunny doorway from sunrise till noon, rapt in reverie, amidst the pines and hickories and sumachs, in undisturbed solitude and stillness, while the birds sang around or flitted noiseless through the house, until by the sun falling in at my west window, or the noise of some traveller's wagon on the distant highway, I was reminded of the lapse of time. I grew in those seasons like corn in the night, and they were far better than any work of the hands would have been. They were not time subtracted from my life, but so much over and above my usual allowance. I realized what the Orientals mean by contemplation and the forsaking of works. For the most part, I minded not how the hours went. The day advanced as if to light some works of mine.

It is evident, from the above-quoted passage, that Thoreau practiced meditation, though in what form and with what regularity, no mention is made in *Walden*.* There is no denying, however, that through his extensive reading in the Oriental classics and his immersion in Eastern philosophy and religion Thoreau discovered an inward mental discipline that harmonized with his physical being. Having thus achieved this inner and outer equilibrium, the mind in contemplation is absorbed in a state of "cosmic consciousness" whereby the self and the universe become One. At this moment—in what Emerson called a "concentrated eternity"—the soul passes through an "invisible boundary" and is emancipated.

_____

* In a letter to a friend, H. G. O. Blake, dated November 20, 1849, however, Thoreau wrote: "Depend upon it that, rude and careless as I am, I would fain practice *the yoga* faithfully." And again, in the same letter: "To some extent, and at rare intervals, even I am a yogi."

Thoreau's religion was not a static thing. "We need," he declared, "to witness our limits transgressed, and some life pasturing freely where we never wander." Thoreau achieved enlightenment on one level by surrendering his conscious self—the false self we call the ego—to his faith in the essential interrelatedness of nature, and so was united with the universe. Thus, in the process of becoming, of moving toward self-realization, the illusion of separateness is eroded. We do not need to become supermen. True faith is transcendent; it transforms both men and things. This is why Thoreau could say, for he believed it: be what you were made. "However mean your life is, meet it and live it; do not shun it and call it hard names. It is not so bad as you are."

Though a Westerner by birth, Thoreau belonged to the Orient in his thought, philosophy, and manner of living. He was closer to Brahma and the Buddha, as he said, than to Moses or Christ. More precisely: he was an eclectic. Through his eclecticism he achieved a synthesis, and that synthesis led to the discovery of god-in-nature. Thoreau *created* god through rooting himself in nature—in reality. Hence the vital emphasis on living in the present, in the here-and-now. To be sure, by rejecting the dogma of "doing good works" as a precondition for entrance to the next life, the man of Walden followed the Eastern path of nonaction in order to free his spirit in *this* life. "I honor you," wrote his friend Harrison Gray Otis Blake, "because you abstain from action, and open your soul that you may *be* somewhat."

Thoreau scholarship has suffered from a need for

greater appreciation of the Eastern philosophy of nonaction and nonattachment, which Thoreau embraced. The author of ''Civil Disobedience'' scorned the so-called social reformers, not because he was weak-willed or lacked conviction, but because he believed that all radical change occurs within. When there has been a revolution effected by the individual in the moral realm, the whole of society is transformed spontaneously. Such was the way he viewed the abolition of slavery in his own lifetime; such was the way he viewed the remedy for the injustices perpetuated by the government and his fellow men. By letting things alone, allowing nature to take its course, the evil will ultimately destroy itself and harmony be once more restored. Nonattachment, Thoreau wrote near the end of his life, alluding to the impending war between the North and South, ''is just the most fatal, and, indeed, the only fatal weapon you can direct against evil, ever.''

Despite the popular portrayal of Thoreau as a recluse, eccentric, and misanthrope, in reality he was none of these. He was no ''hater of mankind'' but affirmed rather, in words he printed for all to read, ''that I love society as much as most, . . . and might sit out the sturdiest frequenter of the bar-room, if my business called me thither.'' Besides situating himself no more than a short distance from town, Thoreau occupied the cabin he built at Walden for only two years; and during the period of his stay he was frequently in contact with ''the outside world.'' If he criticized his contemporaries, as he did, it was not with malice but for love of truth and justice—he would not settle for less and demanded no less of himself. In a real sense, "No truer American existed than Thoreau." As Emerson closed his eulogy of Thoreau some hundred-odd years ago, so it still appears fitting to repeat his words here:

> The country knows not yet, or in the least part, how great a son it has lost. It seems an injury that he should leave in the midst his broken task, which none else can finish,—a kind of indignity to so noble a soul, that he should depart out of Nature before yet he has been really shown to his peers for what he is. But he, at least, is content. His soul was made for the noblest society; he had in a short life exhausted the capabilities of this world; wherever there is knowledge, wherever there is virtue, wherever there is beauty, he will find a home.

To posterity Thoreau has given his writings and in the thoughts, truly, is the man.

WHO I AM

I should not talk so much about myself if there were anybody else whom I knew as well. Unfortunately, I am confined to this theme by the narrowness of my experience. Moreover, I, on my side, require of every writer, first or last, a simple and sincere account of his own life, and not merely what he has heard of other men's lives; some such account as he would send to his kindred from a distant land; for if he has lived sincerely, it must have been in a distant land to me.

Walden, "Economy"

I am as unfit for any practical purpose—I mean for the furtherance of the world's ends—as gossamer for ship-timber; and I, who am going to be a pencil-maker tomorrow, can sympathize with God Apollo, who served King Admetus for a while on earth. But I believe he found it for his advantage at last,—as I am sure I shall, though I shall hold the nobler part at least out of the service.

Correspondence, To Mrs. Lucy Brown, September 8, 1841

I am a Schoolmaster—a Private Tutor, a Surveyor—a Gardener, a Farmer—a Painter, I mean a House Painter, a Carpenter, a Mason, a Day-Laborer, a Pencil-Maker, a Glass-paper Maker, a Writer, and sometimes a Poet-aster. If you will act the part of Iolas, and apply a hot

1

iron to any of these heads, I shall be greatly obliged to you.

Correspondence, To Henry Williams, Jr.,
September 30, 1847

. . . though I could state to a select few that department of human inquiry which engages me, and should be rejoiced at an opportunity to do so, I felt that it would be to make myself the laughing-stock of the scientific community to describe or attempt to describe to them that branch of science which specially interests me, inasmuch as they do not believe in a science which deals with the higher law. So I was obliged to speak to their condition and describe to them that poor part of me which alone they can understand. The fact is I am a mystic, a transcendentalist, and a natural philosopher to boot. Now I think of it, I should have told them at once that I was a transcendentalist. That would have been the shortest way of telling them that they would not understand my explanations.

Journal, March 5, 1853

My profession is to be always on the alert to find God in nature, to know his lurking-places, to attend all the oratorios, the operas, in nature.

Journal, September 7, 1851

There is some advantage in being the humblest, cheapest, least dignified man in the village, so that the very stable boys shall damn you. Methinks I enjoy that advantage to an unusual extent.

Journal, July 6, 1851

I went to the woods because I wished to live deliberately, to front only the essential facts of life, and see if I could not learn what it had to teach, and not, when I came to die, discover that I had not lived. I did not wish to live what was not life, living is so dear; nor did I wish to practise resignation, unless it was quite necessary. I wanted to live deep and suck out all the marrow of life, to live so sturdily and Spartan-like as to put to rout all that was not life, to cut a broad swath and shave close, to drive life into a corner, and reduce it to its lowest terms, and, if it proved to be mean, why then to get the whole and genuine meanness of it, and publish its meanness to the world; or if it were sublime, to know it by experience, and be able to give a true account of it in my next excursion. For most men, it appears to me, are in a strange uncertainty about it, whether it is of the devil or of God, and have *somewhat hastily* concluded that it is the chief end of man here to ''glorify God and enjoy him forever.''

Walden, ''Where I lived''

But why I changed? why I left the woods? I do not think that I can tell. I have often wished myself back. I do not know any better how I ever came to go there. Perhaps it is none of my business, even if it is yours. Perhaps I wanted a change. There was a little stagnation, it may be. About 2 o'clock in the afternoon the world's axle creaked as if it needed greasing, as if the oxen labored with the wain and could hardly get their load over the ridge of the day. Perhaps if I lived there much longer, I might live there forever.

Journal, January 22, 1852

My faults are:—
Paradoxes,—saying just the opposite,—a style which
    may be imitated.
Ingenious.
Playing with words,—getting the laugh,—not always
    simple, strong, and broad.
Using current phrases and maxims, when I should
    speak for myself.
Not always earnest.
"In short," "in fact," "alas!" etc.
Want of conciseness.

Journal, September 2, 1854

MAN

I think that the existence of man in nature is the divinest and most startling of all facts. It is a fact which few have realized.

Journal, May 21, 1851

The perfect man has both genius and talent. The one is his head, the other his foot; by one he is, by the other he lives.

Journal, February 13, 1840

It takes a man to make a room silent.

Journal, February 9, 1839

O for a man who is a *man,* and, as my neighbor says, has a bone in his back which you cannot pass your hand through!

Miscellanies, ''Civil Disobedience''

Man is the artificer of his own happiness.

Journal, January 21, 1838

Why should we be in such desperate haste to succeed and in such desperate enterprises? If a man does not keep pace with his companions, perhaps it is because he hears a different drummer. Let him step to the music which he hears, however measured or far away.

Walden, ''Conclusion''

Man is but the place where I stand, and the prospect hence is infinite. It is not a chamber of mirrors which reflect me. When I reflect, I find that there is other than me. Man is a past phenomenon to philosophy. The universe is larger than enough for man's abode. Some rarely go outdoors, most are always at home at night, very few indeed have stayed out all night once in their lives, fewer still have gone behind the world of humanity, seen its institutions like toadstools by the wayside.

Journal, April 2, 1852

A man does best when he is most himself.

Journal, January 21, 1852

For a man to act himself, he must be perfectly free; otherwise, he is in danger of losing all sense of responsibility or of self-respect.

Correspondence, To Helen Thoreau, October 27, 1837

. . . any man more right than his neighbors constitutes a majority of one already.

Miscellanies, "Civil Disobedience"

Self-Realization

First of all a man must see, before he can say.

Journal, November 1, 1851

. . . Go not to any foreign theater for spectacles, but consider first that there is nothing which can delight or astonish the eyes, but you may discover it all in yourselves.

Reform Papers, ''Reform and Reformers''

I learned this, at least, by my experiment; that if one advances confidently in the direction of his dreams, and endeavors to live the life which he has imagined, he will meet with a success unexpected in common hours. He will put some things behind, will pass an invisible boundary; new, universal, and more liberal laws will begin to establish themselves around and within him; or the old laws be expanded, and interpreted in his favor in a more liberal sense, and he will live with the license of a higher order of beings.

Walden, ''Conclusion''

My practice is ''nowhere,'' my opinion is here.

Walden, ''Higher Laws''

If you can speak what you will never hear, if you can write what you will never read, you have done rare things.

A Week, ''Thursday''

It is easier to discover another such a new world as Columbus did, than to go within one fold of this which we appear to know so well; . . .

A Week, ''Friday''

For an impenetrable shield, stand inside yourself.

Journal, June 27, 1840

Every man has to learn the points of compass again as often as he awakes, whether from sleep or any abstraction. Not till we are lost, in other words, not till we have lost the world, do we begin to find ourselves, and realize where we are and the infinite extent of our relations.

Walden, "The Village"

Some are dinning in our ears that we Americans, and moderns generally, are intellectual dwarfs compared with the ancients, or even the Elizabethan men. But what is that to the purpose? A living dog is better than a dead lion. Shall a man go and hang himself because he belongs to the race of pygmies, and not be the biggest pygmy that he can? Let every one mind his own business, and endeavor to be what he was made.

Walden, "Conclusion"

What was the meaning of that South-Sea Exploring Expedition, with all its parade and expense, but an indirect recognition of the fact, that there are continents and seas in the moral world, to which every man is an isthmus or an inlet, yet unexplored by him, but that it is easier to sail many thousand miles through cold and storm and cannibals, in a government ship, with five hundred men and boys to assist one, than it is to explore the private sea, the Atlantic and Pacific Ocean of one's being alone.

Walden, "Conclusion"

I delight to come to my bearings,—not walk in procession with pomp and parade, in a conspicuous place, but to walk even with the Builder of the universe, if I may,—

not to live in this restless, nervous, bustling, trivial
Nineteenth Century, but stand or sit thoughtfully while
it goes by.

Walden, ''Conclusion''

I do not say that John or Jonathan will realize all this;
but such is the character of that morrow which mere
lapse of time can never make to dawn. The light which
puts out our eyes is darkness to us. Only that day dawns
to which we are awake. There is more day to dawn. The
sun is but a morning star.

Walden, ''Conclusion''

Men and Women

The mass of men lead lives of quiet desperation.

Walden, ''Economy''

It is with men as with trees; you must grow slowly to last
long.

Journal, October 29, 1860

There is a stronger desire to be respectable to one's
neighbors than to one's self.

Journal, 1845–47, undated

Do not speak for other men; speak for yourself.

Journal, December 25, 1851

The greatest compliment that was ever paid me was
when one asked me what *I thought,* and attended to my

answer. . . . Commonly, if men want anything of me, it is only to know how many acres I make of their land,—since I am a surveyor,—or, at most, what trivial news I have burdened myself with. They never will go to law for my meat; they prefer the shell.

Miscellanies, ''Life Without Principle''

The greater part of what my neighbors call good I believe in my soul to be bad, and if I repent of anything, it is very likely to be my good behavior. What demon possessed me that I behaved so well?

Walden, ''Economy''

The mass never comes up to the standard of its best member, but on the contrary degrades itself to a level with the lowest. As the reformers say, it is a levelling down, not up. Hence the mass is only another name for the mob.

Journal, March 14, 1838

How much of the life of certain men *goes* to sustain, to make respected, the institutions of society. They are the ones who pay the heaviest tax.

Journal, September 6, 1851

Nowadays, men wear a fool's cap, and call it a liberty-cap.

Miscellanies, ''Slavery in Massachusetts''

The practice of giving the feminine gender—to all ideal excellence personified, is a mark of refinement, observable in the mythologies even of the most barbarous nations.

10

Glory and victory even are of the feminine gender, but it takes manly qualities to gain them. Man is masculine, but his manliness (virtue) feminine. It is the inclination of brute force to moral power.

Consciousness in Concord

A man of fine perceptions is more truly feminine than a merely sentimental woman.

Familiar Letter, To H. G. O. Blake, September, 1852

It is remarkable, but nevertheless true, as far as my observation goes, that women, to whom we commonly concede a somewhat finer and more sibylline nature, yield a more implicit obedience even to their animal instincts than men. The nature in them is stronger, the reason weaker. . . . I think that the reformer of the severest, as well as finest, class will find more sympathy in the intellect and philosophy of man than in the refinement and delicacy of woman. It is, perchance, a part of woman's conformity and easy nature. Her savior must not be too strong, stern, and intellectual, but charitable above all things.

Journal, November 2, 1850

Society

In society you will not find health, but in nature. Unless our feet at least stood in the midst of nature, all our faces would be pale and livid. Society is always diseased, and the best is the most so.

Excursions, "Natural History of Massachusetts"

Most revolutions in society have not power to interest, still less alarm us; but tell me that our rivers are drying up, or the genus pine dying out in the country, and I might attend.

A Week, ''Monday''

. . . wherever a man goes, men will pursue and paw him with their dirty institutions, and, if they can, constrain him to belong to their desperate odd-fellow society. It is true, I might have resisted forcibly with more or less effect, might have run ''amok'' against society; but I preferred that society should run ''amok'' against me, it being the desperate party.

Walden, ''The Village''

Nations are possessed with an insane ambition to perpetuate the memory of themselves by the amount of hammered stone they leave. What if equal pains were taken to smooth and polish their manners? One piece of good sense would be more memorable than a monument, as high as the moon.

Walden, ''Economy''

Tell me some truth about society and you will annihilate it.

Reform Papers, ''Reform and the Reformers''

Society is commonly too cheap. We meet at very short intervals, not having had time to acquire any new value for each other. We meet at meals three times a day, and give each other a new taste of that old musty cheese that we are. We have had to agree on a certain set of rules, called etiquette and politeness, to make this frequent meeting tolerable and that we need not come to open war. . . . We live thick and are in each other's way, and stumble over one another, and I think that we thus lose some respect for one another. Certainly less frequency would suffice for all important and hearty communications. . . . It would be better if there were but one inhabitant to a square mile, as where I live. The value of a man is not in his skin, that we should touch him.

Walden, ''Solitude''

For my part, I could easily do without the post-office. I think that there are very few important communications made through it. To speak critically, I never received more than one or two letters in my life—I wrote this some years ago—that were worth the postage.

Walden, ''Where I lived''

I sometimes reproach myself because I do not find anything attractive in certain mere trivial employments of men,—that I skip men so commonly, and their affairs,— the professions and the trades,—do not elevate them at least in my thought and get some material for poetry out of them directly. I will not avoid, then, to go by where these men are repairing the stone bridge,—see if I cannot see poetry in that, if that will not yield me a reflection. It is narrow to be confined to woods and fields and grand aspects of nature only. The greatest and wisest will still be related to men. Why not see men standing in the sun and casting a shadow, even as trees? May not

13

some light be reflected from them as from the stems of trees? I will try to enjoy them as animals, at least. They are perhaps better animals than men.

Journal, August 23, 1851

If I should sell both my forenoons and afternoons to society, as most appear to do, I am sure that for me there would be nothing left worth living for. I trust that I shall never thus sell my birthright for a mess of pottage.

Miscellanies, "Life Without Principle"

There is a solid bottom everywhere. We read that the traveller asked the boy if the swamp before him had a hard bottom. The boy replied that it had. But presently the traveller's horse sank in up to the girths, and he observed to the boy, "I thought you said that this bog had a hard bottom." "So it has," answered the latter, "but you have not got half way to it yet." So it is with the bogs and quicksands of society; but he is an old boy that knows it.

Walden, "Conclusion"

As for these [utopian] communities, I think I had rather keep bachelor's hall in hell than go to board in heaven. Do you think your virtue will be boarded with you?

Journal, March 3, 1841

All nations love the same jests and tales, Jews, Christians, and Mahometans, and the same translated suffice for all. All men are children, and of one family.

A Week, "Sunday"

I rejoice that horses and steers have to be broken before they can be made the slaves of men, and that men themselves have some wild oats still left to sow before they become submissive members of society.

Excursions, ''Walking''

Friendship

. . . Nature has many rhymes, but friendship is the most heroic of all.

Consciousness in Concord

Think of the importance of Friendship in the education of men.

"He that hath love and judgment too,
Sees more than any other doe."

It will make a man honest; it will make him a hero; it will make him a saint. It is the state of the just dealing with the just, the magnanimous with the magnanimous, the sincere with the sincere, man with man.

A Week, ''Wednesday''

As I love nature, as I love singing birds, and gleaming stubble, and flowing rivers, and morning and evening, and summer and winter, I love thee, my Friend.

A Week, ''Wednesday''

The most I can do for my friend is simply to be his friend. I have no wealth to bestow on him. If he knows

15

that I am happy in loving him, he will want no other reward. Is not Friendship divine in this?

Journal, February 7, 1841

No word is oftener on the lips of men than Friendship, and indeed no thought is more familiar to their aspirations. All men are dreaming of it, and its drama, which is always a tragedy, is enacted daily. It is the secret of the universe.

A Week, "Wednesday"

We must accept or refuse one another as we are. I could tame a hyena more easily than my Friend. He is a material which no tool of mine will work.

A Week, "Wednesday"

See what a swift penalty you have to pay. If you say to your friend that he is less than an angel, he is your friend no longer.

Journal, January 31, 1852

My friend must be my tent companion.

Consciousness in Concord

All romance is grounded on friendship.

Journal, February 18, 1840

Solitude

I love to be alone. I never found the companion that was so companionable as solitude.

Walden, "Solitude"

I have never felt lonesome, or in the least oppressed by a sense of solitude, but once, and that was a few weeks after I came to the woods, when, for an hour, I doubted if the near neighborhood of man was not essential to a serene and healthy life. To be alone was something unpleasant. But I was at the same time conscious of a slight insanity in my mood, and seemed to foresee my recovery. In the midst of a gentle rain while these thoughts prevailed, I was suddenly sensible of such sweet and beneficent society in Nature, in the very pattering of the drops, and in every sound and sight around my house, an infinite and unaccountable friendliness all at once like an atmosphere sustaining me, as made the fancied advantages of human neighborhood insignificant, and I have never thought of them since. Every little pine needle expanded and swelled with sympathy and befriended me. I was so distinctly made aware of the presence of something kindred to me, even in scenes which we are accustomed to call wild and dreary, and also that the nearest of blood to me and humanest was not a person nor a villager, that I thought no place could ever be strange to me again.

Walden, "Solitude"

I have a great deal of company in my house; especially in the morning, when nobody calls.

Walden, "Solitude"

It is a great relief when for a few moments in the day we can retire to our chamber and be completely true to ourselves. It leavens the rest of our hours.

Journal, March 20, 1841

I have found that no exertion of the legs can bring two minds much nearer to one another.

Walden, "Solitude"

The farmer can work alone in the field or the woods all day, hoeing or chopping, and not feel lonesome, because he is employed; but when he comes home at night he cannot sit down in a room alone, at the mercy of his thoughts, but must be where he can "see the folks," and recreate, and, as he thinks, remunerate himself for his day's solitude; and hence he wonders how the student can sit alone in the house all night and most of the day without ennui and "the blues;" but he does not realize that the student, though in the house, is still at work in *his* field, and chopping in *his* woods, as the farmer in his, and in turn seeks the same recreation and society that the latter does, though it may be a more condensed form of it.

Walden, "Solitude"

You think that I am impoverishing myself by withdrawing from men, but in my solitude I have woven for myself a silken web or *chrysalis,* and, nymph-like, shall ere long burst forth a more perfect creature, fitted for a higher society.

Journal, February 8, 1857

Love

What is the singing of birds, or any natural sound, compared with the voice of one we love?

Journal, April 30, 1851

Love is a mutual confidence whose foundations no one knows. The one I love surpasses all the laws of nature in sureness. Love is capable of any wisdom.

Journal, April 30, 1851

Love is the wind, the tide, the waves, the sunshine. Its power is incalculable; it is many horse-power. It never ceases, it never slacks; it can move the globe without a resting-place; it can warm without fire; it can feed without meat; it can clothe without garments; it can shelter without roof; it can make a paradise within which will dispense with a paradise without.

Reform Papers, "Paradise (to Be) Regained"

Let Love be purified, and all the rest will follow. A pure love is thus, indeed, the panacea for all the ills of the world.

Familiar Letters, To H. G. O. Blake,
September, 1852

Love is the profoundest of secrets. Divulged, even to the beloved, it is no longer Love. As if it were merely I that loved you. When love ceases, then it is divulged.

Familiar Letters, To H. G. O. Blake,
September, 1852

Love does not analyze its object.

Journal, September 14, 1841

Love must be as much a light as a flame.

Familiar Letters, To H. G. O. Blake,
September, 1852

Those whom we can love, we can hate; to others we are indifferent.

Journal, February 24, 1857

There is no remedy for love but to love more.

Journal, July 25, 1839

Marriage

To be married at least should be the one poetical act of a man's life. If you fail in this respect, in what respect will you succeed? The marriage which the mass of men comprehend is but little better than the marriage of the beasts. It would be just as fit for such a man to discourse to you on the love of flowers, thinking of them as hay for his oxen.

Journal, August 11, 1853

If common sense had been consulted, how many marriages would never have taken place; if uncommon or divine sense, how few marriages such as we witness would ever have taken place!

Familiar Letters, To H. G. O. Blake,
September, 1852

I am sure that the design of my maker when he has brought me nearest to woman was not the propagation, but rather the maturation, of the species. Man is capable of a love of woman quite transcending marriage.

Journal, April 30, 1851

If it is the result of a pure love, there can be nothing sensual in marriage. Chastity is something positive, not negative. It is the virtue of the married especially. All lusts or base pleasures must give place to loftier delights.

Familiar Letters, To H. G. O. Blake,
September, 1852

Chastity

Each man's mode of speaking of the sexual relation proves how sacred his own relations of that kind are. We do not respect the mind that can jest on this subject.

Journal, March 4, 1852

I lose my respect for the man who can make the mystery of sex the subject of a coarse jest, yet, when you speak earnestly and seriously on the subject, is silent. I feel that this is to be truly irreligious. Whatever may befall me, I trust that I may never lose my respect for purity in others. The subject of sex is one on which I do not wish to meet a man at all unless I *can* meet him on the most inspiring ground,—if his view degrades, and does not elevate. I would preserve purity in act and thought, as I would cherish the memory of my mother. A companion can possess no worse quality than vulgarity. If I find that *he* is not habitually reverent of the fact of sex, I, even I, will not associate with [him].* I will cast this first stone.

Journal, April 12, 1852

---

* Brackets appear in the original.

Bravery

The strongest is always the least violent.

Reform Papers, ''The Service''

A brave soul will make these peaceful times danger-ous—and dangerous times peaceful.

Consciousness in Concord

A brave man always knows the way, no matter how in-tricate the roads.

Journal, February 7, 1841

Bravery and Cowardice are kindred correlatives with Knowledge and Ignorance, Light and Darkness, Good and Evil.

Journal, December, 1839, undated

When were the good and the brave ever in a majority?

Miscellanies, ''A Plea for John Brown''

No doubt you can get more in your market for a quart of milk than for a quart of blood, but that is not the market that heroes carry their blood to.

Miscellanies, ''A Plea for John Brown''

My Contemporaries

John Brown

No man in America has ever stood up so persistently and effectively for the dignity of human nature, knowing

himself for a man, and the equal of any and all govern-
ments. In that sense he was the most American of us all.
Miscellanies, ''A Plea for John Brown''

When a man stands up serenely against the condemna-
tion and vengeance of mankind, rising above them
literally *by a whole body,*—even though he were of late
the vilest murderer, who has settled that matter with
himself,—the spectacle is a sublime one,—didn't ye
know it, ye *Liberators,* ye *Tribunes,* ye *Republicans?*—
and we become criminal in comparison. Do yourselves
the honor to recognize him. He needs none of your
respect.
Miscellanies, ''A Plea for John Brown''

When we heard at first that he was dead, one of my
townsmen observed that ''he died as the fool dieth;''
which, pardon me, for an instant suggested a likeness in
him dying to my neighbor living. Others, craven-
hearted, said disparagingly, that ''he threw his life
away,'' because he resisted the government. Which way
have they thrown *their* lives, pray?
Miscellanies, ''A Plea for John Brown''

Ralph Waldo Emerson

Emerson again is a critic, poet, philosopher, with talent
not so conspicuous, not so adequate to his task; but his
field is still higher, his task more arduous. Lives a far
more intense life; seeks to realize a divine life; his affections and intellect equally developed. Has advanced farther, and a new heaven opens to him. Love and Friend-

23

ship, Religion, Poetry, the Holy are familiar to him. The life of an Artist; more variegated, more observing, finer perception; not so robust, elastic; practical enough in his own field; faithful, a judge of men. There is no such general critic of men and things, no such trustworthy and faithful man. More of the divine realized in him than in any. A poetic critic, reserving the unqualified nouns for the gods.

Journal, 1845–47, undated

Thomas Carlyle

Carlyle's are not, in the common sense, works of art in their origin and aim; and yet, perhaps, no living English writer evinces an equal literary talent. They are such works of art only as the plow and corn-mill and steam-engine,—not as pictures and statues. Others speak with greater emphasis to scholars, as such, but none so earnestly and effectually to all who can read. . . . He does not need to husband his pearl, but excels by a greater humanity and sincerity.

Miscellanies, ''Carlyle and His Works''

Henry James

I have been to see Henry James, and like him very much. It was a great pleasure to meet him. It makes humanity seem more erect and respectable. I never was more kindly and faithfully catechised. . . . He is a man, and takes his own way, or stands still in his own place. I know of no one so patient and determined to have the good of you. It is almost friendship, such plain and human dealing.

Correspondence, To R. W. Emerson,
June 8, 1843

Walt Whitman

He is apparently the greatest democrat the world has seen. Kings and aristocracy go by the board at once, as they have long deserved to. A remarkably strong though coarse nature, of a sweet disposition, and much prized by his friends. Though peculiar and rough in his exterior, . . . he is essentially a gentleman.

Correspondence, To H. G. O. Blake,
November 19, 1856

Mrs. R. W. (Lydian) Emerson

I shall not hesitate to know you. I think of you as some elder sister of mine, whom I could not have avoided,—a sort of lunar influence,—only of such age as the moon, whose time is measured by her light. You must know that you represent to me woman, for I have not traveled very far or wide,—and what if I had? I like to deal with you, for I believe you do not lie or steal, and these are very rate virtues. I thank you for your influence for two years. I was fortunate to be subjected to it, and am now to remember it. It is the noblest gift we can make; what signify all others that can be bestowed?

Correspondence, To Mrs. R. W. Emerson,
May 22, 1843

Bronson Alcott

Alcott is a geometer, a visionary, the Laplace of ethics, more intellect, less of the affections, sight beyond talents, a substratum of practical skill and knowledge unquestionable, but overlaid and concealed by a faith in the unseen and impracticable. Seeks to realize an entire life; a catholic observer; habitually takes in the farthest star and nebula into his scheme. Will be the last man to be disappointed as the ages revolve. His attitude is one of greater faith and expectation than that of any man I know; with little to show; with undue share, for a philosopher, of the weaknesses of humanity. The most hospital intellect, embracing high and low. For children how much that means, for the insane and vagabond, for the poet and scholar!

Journal, 1845–47, undated

William Ellery Channing

In our walks C[hanning] takes out his note-book sometimes and tries to write as I do, but all in vain. He soon puts it up again, or contents himself with scrawling some sketch of the landscape. Observing me still scribbling, he will say that he confines himself to the ideal, purely ideal remarks; he leaves the facts to me. Sometimes, too, he will say a little petulantly, "*I* am universal; I have nothing to do with the particular and definite." He is the moodiest person, perhaps, that I ever saw. As naturally whimsical as a cow is brindled, both in his tenderness and his roughness he belies himself. He can be incredibly selfish and unexpectedly generous. He is conceited, and yet there is in him far more than usual to ground conceit upon.

Journal, November 9, 1851

George Minott

Minott is, perhaps, the most poetical farmer—who most realizes to me the poetry of the farmer's life—that I know. He does nothing with haste and drudgery, but as if he loved it. He makes the most of his labor, and takes infinite satisfaction in every part of it. . . .

He loves to walk in a swamp in windy weather and hear the wind groan through the pines. . . . He indulges in no luxury of food or dress or furniture, yet he is not penurious but merely simple. If his sister dies before him, he may have to go to the almshouse in his old age; yet he is not poor, for he does not want riches. . . . With never-failing rheumatism and trembling hands, he seems yet to enjoy perennial health.

Journal, October 4, 1851

Mary Emerson

Just spent a couple of hours (eight to ten) with Miss Mary Emerson at Holbrook's. The wittiest and most vivacious woman that I know, certainly that woman among my acquaintance whom it is most profitable to meet, the least frivolous, who will most surely provoke to good conversation and the expression of what is in you. She is singular, among women at least, in being really and perseveringly interested to know what thinkers think. She relates herself surely to the intellectual where she goes. It is perhaps her greatest praise and peculiarity that she, more surely than any other woman, gives her companion occasion to utter his best thought. . . . In short, she is a genius, as woman seldom is, reminding you less often of her sex than any woman whom I know. . . . I never talked with any other woman who I thought accompanied me so far in describing a poetic experience. Miss Fuller is the only woman I think of in this connection, and of her rather from her fame than from any knowledge of her. Miss Emerson expressed to-night a singular want of respect for her own sex, saying that they were frivolous almost without exception, that woman was the weaker vessel, etc.; that into whatever family she might go, she depended more upon the "clown" for society than upon the lady of the house. Men are more likely to have opinions of their own.

Journal, November 13, 1851

LIFE

However mean your life is, meet it and live it; do not shun it and call it hard names. It is not so bad as you are. It looks poorest when you are richest. The fault-finder will find faults even in paradise.

Walden, ''Conclusion''

I long ago lost a hound, a bay horse, and a turtledove, and am still on their trail. Many are the travellers I have spoken to concerning them, describing their tracks and what calls they answered to. I have met one or two who had heard the hound, and the tramp of the horse, and even seen the dove disappear behind a cloud, and they seemed as anxious to recover them as if they had lost them themselves.

Walden, ''Economy''

Why should we not meet, not always as dyspeptics, to tell our bad dreams, but sometimes as *eu*peptics, to congratulate each other on the ever-glorious morning? I do not make an exorbitant demand, surely.

Miscellanies, ''Life Without Principle''

Give me the obscure life, the cottage of the poor and humble, the workdays of the world, the barren fields, the smallest share of all things but poetic perception. Give me but the eyes to see the things which you possess.

Journal, August 28, 1851

The necessaries of life for man in this climate may, accurately enough, be distributed under the several heads of Food, Shelter, Clothing, and Fuel; for not till we have secured these are we prepared to entertain the true problems of life with freedom and a prospect of success.

Walden, ''Economy''

. . . if you are restricted in your range by poverty, if you cannot buy books and newspapers, for instance, you are but confined to the most significant and vital experiences; you are compelled to deal with the material which yields the most sugar and the most starch. It is life near the bone where it is sweetest.

Walden, ''Conclusion''

Be it life or death, we crave only reality. If we are really dying, let us hear the rattle in our throats and feel cold in the extremities; if we are alive, let us go about our business.

Walden, ''Where I lived''

My desire is to know *what* I have lived, that I may know *how* to live henceforth.

Journal, November 12, 1837

I love a broad margin to my life.

Walden, ''Sounds''

Wherever I sat, there I might live, and the landscape radiated from me accordingly.

Walden, ''Where I Lived''

I would not have any one adopt *my* mode of living on any account; for, beside that before he has fairly learned it I may have found out another for myself, I desire that there may be as many different persons in the world as possible; but I would have each one be very careful to find out and pursue *his own* way, and not his father's or his mother's or his neighbor's instead.

Walden, ''Economy''

Life consists with wildness. The most alive is the wildest.

Excursions, ''Walking''

Simplicity

In proportion as he simplifies his life, the laws of the universe will appear less complex, and solitude will not be solitude, nor poverty poverty, nor weakness weakness. If you have built castles in the air, your work need not be lost; that is where they should be. Now put the foundations under them.

Walden, ''Conclusion''

Our life is frittered away by detail. An honest man has hardly need to count more than his ten fingers, or in extreme cases he may add his ten toes, and lump the rest. Simplicity, simplicity, simplicity! I say, let your affairs be as two or three, and not a hundred or a thousand; instead of a million count half a dozen, and keep your accounts on your thumb-nail.

Walden, ''Where I Lived''

Simplify, simplify. Instead of three meals a day, if it be necessary eat but one; instead of a hundred dishes, five; and reduce other things in proportion.

Walden, "Where I Lived"

There are two kinds of simplicity,—one that is akin to foolishness, the other to wisdom. The philosopher's style of living is only outwardly simple, but inwardly complex. The savage's style is both outwardly and inwardly simple. A simpleton can perform many mechanical labors, but is not capable of profound thought. It was their limited view, not in respect to *style*, but to the *object* of living. A man who has equally limited views with respect to the end of living will not be helped by the most complex and refined style of living. It is not the tub that makes Diogenes, the Jove-born, but Diogenes the tub.

Journal, September 1, 1853

Money

I should like not to exchange *any* of my life for money.

Correspondence, To H. G. O. Blake,
December 31, 1856

Superfluous wealth can buy superfluities only. Money is not required to buy one necessary of the soul.

Walden, "Conclusion"

No man is rich enough to keep a poet in his pay.

Journal, March 20, 1858

Almost any man knows how to earn money, but not one in a million knows how to spend it. If he had known so much as this, he would never have earned it.

Journal, 1837–47, undated.

The ways by which you may get money almost without exception lead downward. To have done anything by which you earned money *merely* is to have been truly idle or worse.

Miscellanies, "Life Without Principle"

The community has no bribe that will tempt a wise man. You may raise money enough to tunnel a mountain, but you cannot raise money enough to hire a man who is minding *his own* business.

Miscellanies, "Life Without Principle"

Absolutely speaking, the more money, the less virtue; for money comes between a man and his objects and obtains them for him; and it was certainly no great virtue to obtain it. . . . The best thing a man can do for his culture when he is rich is to endeavor to carry out those schemes which he entertained when he was poor.

Miscellanies, "Civil Disobedience"

Merely to come into the world the heir of a fortune is not to be born, but to be still-born, rather.

Miscellanies, "Life Without Principle"

A man had better starve at once than lose his innocence in the process of getting his bread.

Miscellanies, "Life Without Principle"

Business and Labor

This world is a place of business. What an infinite bustle! I am awaked almost every night by the panting of the locomotive. It interrupts my dreams. There is no sabbath. It would be glorious to see mankind at leisure for once. It is nothing but work, work, work. I cannot easily buy a blank-book to write thoughts in; they are commonly ruled for dollars and cents. An Irishman, seeing me making a minute in the fields, took it for granted that I was calculating my wages. If a man was tossed out of a window when an infant, and so made a cripple for life, or scared out of his wits by the Indians, it is regretted chiefly because he was thus incapacitated for—business! I think that there is nothing, not even crime, more opposed to poetry, to philosophy, ay, to life itself, than this incessant business.

Miscellanies, "Life Without Principle"

This spending of the best part of one's life earning money in order to enjoy a questionable liberty during the least valuable part of it reminds me of the Englishman who went to India to make a fortune first, in order that he might return to England and live the life of a poet. He should have gone up garret at once.

Walden, "Economy"

If a man walk in the woods for love of them half of each day, he is in danger of being regarded as a loafer; but if he spends his whole day as a speculator, shearing off those woods and making earth bald before her time, he is esteemed an industrious and enterprising citizen. As if a town had no interest in its forests but to cut them down!

Miscellanies, "Life Without Principle"

There are certain current expressions and blasphemous moods of viewing things, as when we say "he is doing a good business," more profane than cursing and swearing. There is death and sin in such words. Let not the children hear them.

Journal, April 20, 1841

. . . unless we do more than simply learn the trade of our time, we are but apprentices, and not yet masters of the art of life.

A Week, "Monday"

Do not hire a man who does your work for money, but him who does it for love of it.

Miscellanies, "Life Without Principle"

The aim of the laborer should be, not to get his living, to get "a good job," but to perform well a certain work; and, even in a pecuniary sense, it would be economy for a town to pay its laborers so well that they would not feel that they were working for low ends, as for a livelihood merely, but for scientific, or even moral ends.

Miscellanies, "Life Without Principle"

If you would avoid uncleanness, and all the sins, work earnestly, though it be at cleaning a stable.

Walden, "Higher Laws"

Men and boys are learning all kinds of trades but how to make *men* of themselves. They learn to make houses, but they are not so well housed, they are not so contented in their houses, as the woodchucks in their holes. What is the use of a house if you haven't got a tolerable planet to put it on? If you can not tolerate the planet it is on?

Correspondence, To H. G. O. Blake,
May 20, 1860

Great thoughts hallow any labor. To-day I earned seventy-five cents heaving manure out of a pen, and made a good bargain of it.

Journal, April 20, 1841

In short, I am convinced, both by faith and experience, that to maintain one's self on this earth is not a hardship but a pastime, if we will live simply and wisely; . . . It is not necessary that a man should earn his living by the sweat of his brow, unless he sweats easier than I do.

Walden, "Economy"

To the conscience of the idle man, the stillness of a placid September day sounds like the din and whirl of a factory. Only employment can still this din in the air.

Journal, September 13, 1852

True Wealth

Give me the poverty that enjoys true wealth.

Walden, "Ponds"

. . . a man is rich in proportion to the number of things which he can afford to let alone.

Walden, "Where I Lived"

Just in proportion to the outward poverty is the inward wealth.

Journal, November 13, 1851

Cultivate poverty like a garden herb, like sage. Do not trouble yourself much to get new things, whether clothes or friends. Turn the old; return to them. Things do not change; we change. Sell your clothes and keep your thoughts. God will see that you do not want society.

Walden, "Conclusion"

It is foolish for a man to accumulate material wealth chiefly, houses and land. Our stock in life, our real estate, is that amount of thought which we have had, which we have thought out. The ground we have thus created is forever pasturage for our thoughts.

Journal, May 1, 1857

If a man has spent all his days about some business, by which he has merely got to be rich, as it is called, *i.e.,* has got much money, many houses and barns and wood-lots, then his life has been a failure, I think; but if he has been trying to better his condition in a higher sense than this, has been trying to invent something, to be some-body—*i.e.,* to invent and get a patent for himself,—so that all may see his originality, though he should never get above board,—and great inventors, you know, commonly die poor,—I shall think him comparatively successful.

Journal, November 29, 1860

I did not know that mankind was suffering for want of gold. I have seen a little of it. I know that it is very malleable, but not so malleable as wit. A grain of gold will gild a great surface, but not so much as a grain of wisdom.

Miscellanies, ''Life Without Principle''

Possessions

Most men appear never to have considered what a house is, and are actually though needlessly poor all their lives because they think that they must have such a one as their neighbors have.

Walden, ''Economy''

When I think of acquiring for myself one of our luxurious dwellings, I am deterred, for, so to speak, the country is not yet adapted to *human* culture, and we are still forced to cut our *spiritual* bread far thinner than our forefathers did their wheaten.

Walden, ''Economy''

I had three chairs in my house; one for solitude, two for friendship, three for society.

Walden, ''Visitors''

I would rather sit on a pumpkin and have it all to myself than be crowded on a velvet cushion.

Walden, "Economy"

I had three pieces of limestone on my desk, but I was terrified to find that they required to be dusted daily, when the furniture of my mind was all undusted still, and I threw them out the window in disgust.

Walden, "Economy"

A lady once offered me a mat, but as I had no room to spare within the house, nor time to spare within or without to shake it, I declined it, preferring to wipe my feet on the sod before my door. It is best to avoid the beginnings of evil.

Walden, "Economy"

It is the luxurious and dissipated who set the fashions which the herd so diligently follow.

Walden, "Economy"

Every generation laughs at the old fashions, but follows religiously the new.

Walden, "Economy"

I say, beware of all enterprises that require new clothes, and not rather a new wearer of clothes.

Walden, "Economy"

Only they who go to soirées and legislative halls must have new coats, coats to change as often as the man

39

changes in them. But if my jacket and trousers, my hat and shoes, are fit to worship God in, they will do; will they not?

Walden, ''Economy''

The walker and naturalist does not wear a hat, or a shoe, or a coat, to be looked at, but for other uses. When a citizen comes to take a walk with me I commonly find that he is lame,—disabled by his shoeing. He is sure to wet his feet, tear his coat, and jam his hat, and the superior qualities of my boots, coat, and hat appear. I once went into the woods with a party for a fortnight. I wore my old and common clothes, which were of Vermont gray. They wore, no doubt, the best they had for such an occasion,—of a fashionable color and quality. I thought that they were a little ashamed of me while we were in the towns. They all tore their clothes badly but myself, and I, who, it chanced, was the only one provided with needles and thread, enabled them to mend them. When we came out of the woods I was the best dressed of any of them.

Journal, March 26, 1860

King James loved his old shoes best. Who does not?
Journal, 1845-47, undated

Gifts

The richest gifts we can bestow are the least marketable.
Correspondence, To R. W. Emerson,
February 12, 1843

A noble person confers no such gift as his whole confidence: none so exalts the giver and the receiver; it produces the truest gratitude.

Correspondence, To R. W. Emerson,
February 12, 1843

If you wish to give a man a sense of poverty, give him a thousand dollars. The next hundred dollars he gets will not be worth more than ten that he used to get. Have pity on him; withhold your gifts.

Journal, January 20, 1856

I know many children to whom I would fain make a present on some one of their birthdays, but they are so far gone in the luxury of presents—have such perfect museums of costly ones—that it would absorb my entire earnings for a year to buy them something which would not be beneath their notice.

Journal, November 5, 1855

Health

Health is the free use and command of all our faculties, and equal development.

Journal, February 14, 1851

Measure your health by your sympathy with morning and spring. If there is no response in you to the awakening of nature,—if the prospect of an early morning walk does not banish sleep, if the warble of the first bluebird does not thrill you,—know that the morning and spring of your life are past. Thus may you feel your pulse.

Journal, February 25, 1859

A healthy man, indeed, is the complement of the seasons, and in winter, summer is in his heart.

Excursions, "Winter Walk"

Men have discovered—or think they have discovered— the salutariness of a few wild things only, and not of all nature. Why, "nature" is but another name for health, and the seasons are but different states of health. Some men think that they are not well in spring, or summer, or autumn, or winter; it is only because they are not *well in* them.

Journal, August 23, 1853

I never feel that I am inspired unless my body is also. . . . They are fatally mistaken who think, while they strive with their minds, that they may suffer their bodies to stagnate in luxury or sloth. The body is the first proselyte the Soul makes. . . . The whole duty of man may be expressed in one line,—Make to yourself a perfect body.

Journal, June 21, 1840

In respect to religion and the healing art, all nations are still in a state of barbarism. In the most civilized countries the priest is still but a Powwow, and the physician a Great Medicine. Consider the deference which is everywhere paid to a doctor's opinion. Nothing more strikingly betrays the credulity of mankind than medicine. Quackery is a thing universal, and universally successful.

A Week, ''Wednesday''

One of the worst effects of sickness even is that it may get one into the *habit* of taking a little something, his bitters or sweets, as if for his bodily good, from time to time, when he does not need it.

Correspondence, To Daniel Ricketson,
October 14, 1861

It is the faith with which we take medicine that cures us. Otherwise we may be cured into greater disease.

Journal, June 27, 1852

Food

I should like to see a man whose diet was berries and nuts alone.

Journal, November 7, 1853

I learned from my two years' experience that it would cost incredibly little trouble to obtain one's necessary food, even in this latitude; that a man may use as simple a diet as the animals, and yet retain health and strength. . . . Yet men have come to such a pass that they frequently starve, not for want of necessaries, but for want of luxuries; and I know a good woman who

43

thinks that her son lost his life because he took to drinking water only.

Walden, ''Economy''

I am glad to have drunk water so long, for the same reason that I prefer the natural sky to an opium-eater's heaven. I would fain keep sober always; and there are infinite degrees of drunkenness.

Walden, ''Higher Laws''

It is hard to provide and cook so simple and clean a diet as will not offend the imagination, but this, I think, is to be fed when we feed the body; they should both sit down at the same table. Yet perhaps this may be done. The fruits eaten temperately need not make us ashamed of our appetites, nor interrupt the worthiest pursuits. But put an extra condiment into your dish, and it will poison you. It is not worth the while to live by rich cookery.

Walden, ''Higher Laws''

The gross feeder is a man in the larva state; and there are whole nations in that condition, nations without fancy or imagination, whose vast abdomens betray them.

Walden, ''Higher Laws''

He who distinguishes the true savor of his food can never be a glutton; he who does not cannot be otherwise. A puritan may go to his brown-bread crust with as gross an appetite as ever an alderman to his turtle.

Walden, ''Higher Laws''

It was fit that I should live on rice, mainly, who loved so well the philosophy of India.

Walden, ''Economy''

Like many of my contemporaries, I had rarely for many years used animal food, or tea, or coffee, etc.; not so much because of any ill effects which I had traced to them, as because they were not agreeable to my imagination. . . . It appeared more beautiful to live low and fare hard in many respects; and though I never did so, I went far enough to please my imagination.

Walden, ''Higher Laws''

The practical objection to animal food in my case was its uncleanness; and besides, when I had caught and cleaned and cooked and eaten my fish, they seemed not to have fed me essentially. It was insignificant and unnecessary, and cost more than it came to.

Walden, ''Higher Laws''

I believe that every man who has ever been earnest to preserve his higher poetic faculties in the best condition has been particularly inclined to abstain from animal food, and from much food of any kind.

Walden, ''Higher Laws''

There is a certain class of unbelievers who sometimes ask me such questions as, if I think that I can live on vegetable food alone; and to strike at the root of the matter at once,—for the root is faith,—I am accustomed to answer such, that I can live on board nails. If they cannot understand that, they cannot understand much that I have to say.

Walden, "Economy"

One farmer says to me, "You cannot live on vegetable food solely, for it furnishes nothing to make bones with;" and so he religiously devotes a part of his day to supplying his system with the raw material of bones; walking all the while he talks behind his oxen, which, with vegetable-made bones, jerk him and his lumbering plow along in spite of every obstacle. Some things are really necessaries of life in some circles, the most helpless and diseased, which in others are luxuries merely, and in others still are entirely unknown.

Walden, "Economy"

Is it not a reproach that man is a carnivorous animal? True, he can and does live, in a great measure, by preying on other animals; but this is a miserable way,—as any one who will go to snaring rabbits, or slaughtering lambs, may learn,—and he will be regarded as a benefactor of his race who shall teach man to confine himself to a more innocent and wholesome diet.

Walden, "Higher Laws"

The repugnance to animal food is not the effect of experience, but is an instinct.

Walden, "Higher Laws"

The Senses

We need pray for no higher heaven than the pure senses can furnish, a *purely* sensuous life. Our present senses are but the rudiments of what they are destined to become.

A Week, "Friday"

The senses of children are unprofaned. Their whole body is one sense; they take a physical pleasure in riding on a rail, they love to teeter. So does the unviolated, the unsophisticated mind derive an inexpressible pleasure from the simplest exercise of thoughts.

Journal, July 7, 1851

I suspect that the child plucks its first flower with an insight into its beauty and significance which the subsequent botanist never retains.

Journal, February 5, 1852

The noblest feature, the eye, is the fairest-colored, the jewel of the body.

Journal, October 24, 1858

Methinks the scent is a more primitive inquisition than the eye, more oracular and trustworthy. When I criticise my own writing, I go by the scent, as it were. The scent reveals, of course, what is concealed from the other senses. By it I detect earthiness.

Journal, May 8, 1852

Dreams

The nearest approach to discovering what we are is in dreams.

Journal, April 27, 1841

. . . in dreams we never deceive ourselves, nor are deceived, . . . Dreams are the touchstones of our characters. . . . Our truest life is when we are in dreams awake.

A Week, ''Wednesday''

In dreams the links of life are united: we forget that our friends are dead; we know them as of old.

Journal, May 23, 1853

Death

A man can attend but one funeral in the course of his life, can behold but one corpse.

Cape Cod, ''Shipwreck''

In proportion as death is more earnest than life, it is better than life.

Journal, October 7, 1857

. . . death is beautiful when seen to be a law, and not an accident—It is as common as life.

Correspondence, To R. W. Emerson,
March 11, 1842

On the death of a friend, we should consider that the fates through confidence have devolved on us the task of a double living, that we have henceforth to fulfill the promise of our friend's life also, in our own, to the world.

Journal, February 28, 1840

What right have I to grieve, who have not ceased to wonder? . . . Only nature has a right to grieve perpetually, for she only is innocent.

Correspondence, To Mrs. Lucy Brown,
March 2, 1842

Nature herself has not provided the most graceful end for her creatures. What becomes of all these birds that people the air and forest for our solacement? The sparrows seem always *chipper*, never infirm. We do not see their bodies lie about. Yet there is a tragedy at the end of each one of their lives.

A Week, "Tuesday"

NATURE

I wish to speak a word for Nature, for absolute freedom and wildness, as contrasted with a freedom and culture merely civil,—to regard man as an inhabitant, or a part and parcel of Nature, rather than a member of society. I wish to make an extreme statement, if so I may make an emphatic one, for there are enough champions of civilization: the minister and the school committee and every one of you will take care of that.

Excursions, ''Walking''

. . . the earth is the mother of all creatures.

Journal, September 9, 1854

I believe that there is a subtle magnetism in Nature, which, if we unconsciously yield to it, will direct us aright.

Excursions, ''Walking''

Let a man have thought what he will of Nature in the house, she will still be novel outdoors. I keep out of doors for the sake of the mineral, vegetable, and animal in me.

Journal, November 4, 1852

Nature is beautiful only as a place where a life is to be lived. It is not beautiful to him who has not resolved on a beautiful life.

Journal, July 21, 1853

Nature must be viewed humanly to be viewed at all; that is, her scenes must be associated with humane affections, such as are associated with one's native place, for instance. She is most significant to a lover. A lover of Nature is preëminently a lover of man. If I have no friend, what is Nature to me? She ceases to be morally significant.

Journal, June 30, 1852

Nature has no human inhabitant who appreciates her. The birds with their plumage and their notes are in harmony with the flowers, but what youth or maiden conspires with the wild luxuriant beauty of Nature? She flourishes most alone, far from the towns where they reside. Talk of heaven! ye disgrace earth.

Walden, ''Ponds''

I love Nature partly *because* she is not man, but a retreat from him. None of his institutions control or pervade her. There a different kind of right prevails. In her midst I can be glad with an entire gladness. If this world were all man, I could not stretch myself, I should lose all hope. He is constraint, she is freedom to me. He makes me wish for another world. She makes me content with this.

Journal, January 3, 1853

The West of which I speak is but another name for the Wild; and what I have been preparing to say is, that in Wildness is the preservation of the World.

Excursions, ''Walking''

There are other, savager and more primeval aspects of Nature than our poets have sung. It is only white man's poetry.

A Week, ''Sunday''

I wish to know an entire heaven and an entire earth. All the great trees and beasts, fishes and fowl are gone. The streams, perchance, are somewhat shrunk.

Journal, March 23, 1856

How rarely a man's love for nature becomes a ruling principle with him, like a youth's affection for a maiden, but more enduring! All nature is my bride. That nature which to one is a stark and ghastly solitude is a sweet, tender, and genial society to another.

Journal, April 23, 1857

It is difficult to conceive of a region uninhabited by man. We habitually presume his presence and influence everywhere. And yet we have not seen pure Nature, unless we have seen her thus vast and drear and in-human, though in the midst of cities. . . . What is it to be admitted to a museum, to see a myriad of particular things, compared with being shown some star's surface, some hard matter in its home!

Maine Woods, ''Ktaadn''

At the same time that we are earnest to explore and learn all things, we require that all things be mysterious and unexplorable, that land and sea be infinitely wild, unsurveyed and unfathomed by us because unfathomable. We can never have enough of nature. We must be refreshed by the sight of inexhaustable vigor, vast and titanic features, the sea-coast with its wrecks, the wilderness with its living and its decaying trees, the thundercloud, and the rain which lasts three weeks and produces freshets. We need to witness our own limits transgressed, and some life pasturing freely where we never wander.

Walden, ''Spring''

I stand in awe of my body, this matter to which I am bound has become so strange to me. I fear not spirits, ghosts, of which I am one,—*that* my body might,—but I fear bodies, I tremble to meet them. What is this Titan that has possession of me? Talk of mysteries! Think of our life in nature,—daily to be shown matter, to come in contact with it,—rocks, trees, wind on our cheeks! the *solid* earth! the *actual* world! the *common sense! Contact! Contact! Who* are we? *Where* are we?

Maine Woods, ''Ktaadn''

He is the richest who has most use for nature as raw material of tropes and symbols with which to describe his life. If these gates of golden willows affect me, they correspond to the beauty and promise of some experience on which I am entering. If I am overflowing with life, am rich in experience for which I lack expression, then nature will be my language full of poetry,—all nature will *fable,* and every natural phenomenon be a myth. The man of science, who is not seeking for expression but for a fact to be expressed merely, studies

53

nature as a dead language. I pray for such inward experience as will make nature significant.

Journal, May 10, 1853

Natural Phenomena

The most beautiful thing in nature is the sun reflected from a tearful cloud.

Journal, September 7, 1851

A sky without clouds is a meadow without flowers, a sea without sails.

Journal, June 24, 1852

The man is blessed who every day is permitted to behold anything so pure and serene as the western sky at sunset, while revolutions vex the world.

Journal, December 27, 1851

11 P.M.—Coming home through the village by this full moonlight, it seems one of the most glorious nights I ever beheld. Though the pure snow is so deep around, the air, by contrast perhaps with the recent days, is mild and even balmy to my senses, and the snow is still sticky to my feet and hands. And the sky is the most glorious blue I ever beheld, even a light blue on some sides, as if I actually saw into day, while small white, fleecy clouds, at long intervals, are drifting from west-northwest to south-southeast. . . . The outlines of the elms were never more distinctly seen than now. It seems a

slighting of the gifts of God to go to sleep now; as if we could better afford to close our eyes to daylight, of which we see so much. Has not this blueness of the sky the same cause with the blueness in the holes in the snow, and in some distant shadows on the snow?—if, indeed, it is true that the sky is bluer in winter when the ground is covered with snow.

Journal, February 4, 1852

There was a glorious lurid sunset to-night, accompanied with many sombre clouds, and when I looked into the west with my head turned, the grass had the same fresh green, and the distant herbage and foliage in the horizon the same dark blue, and the clouds and sky the same bright colors beautifully mingled and dissolving into one another, that I have seen in pictures of tropical landscapes and skies. Pale saffron skies with faint fishes of rosy clouds dissolving in them. A bloodstained sky. . . . What shall we make of the fact that you have only to stand on your head a moment to be enchanted with the beauty of the landscape?

Journal, 1850, undated

Is not the rainbow a faint vision of God's face? How glorious should be the life of man passed under this arch! What more remarkable phenomenon than a rainbow, yet how little it is remarked!

Journal, June 22, 1852

The rainbow, after all, does not attract an attention proportionate to its singularity and beauty. . . . What form of beauty could be imagined more striking and conspicuous? An arch of the most brilliant and glorious colors completely spanning [the]* heavens before the eyes of men! Children look at it. It is wonderful that all men do not take pains to behold it. . . . All men beholding it begin to understand the significance of the Greek epithet applied to the world,—name for the world,—*Kosmos,* or beauty. It was designed to impress man. We live, as it were, within the calyx of a flower.

Journal, August 6, 1852

The use of the rainbow, who has described it?

Journal, August 7, 1852

Oceans, Rivers, and Lakes

The ocean is but a larger lake.

Cape Cod, ''The Beach Again''

The river is my own highway, the only wild and unfenced part of the world hereabouts.

Journal, May 30, 1852

Rivers must have been the guides which conducted the footsteps of the first travellers. They are the constant lure, when they flow by our doors, to distant enterprise

---

* Brackets appear in the original.

and adventure; and, by a natural impulse, the dwellers on their banks will at length accompany their currents to the lowlands of the globe, or explore at their invitation the interior of continents. They are the natural highways of all nations, not only levelling the ground and removing obstacles from the path of the traveller, quenching his thirst and bearing him on their bosoms, but conducting him through the most interesting scenery, the most populous portions of the globe, and where the animal and vegetable kingdoms attain their greatest perfection.

A Week, ''Concord River''

The Musketaquid, or Grass-ground River, though probably as old as the Nile or Euphrates, did not begin to have a place in civilized history until the fame of its grassy meadows and its fish attracted settlers out of England in 1635, when it received the other but kindred name of CONCORD from the first plantation on its banks, which appears to have been commenced in a spirit of peace and harmony. It will be Grass-ground River as long as grass grows and water runs here; it will be Concord River only while men lead peaceable lives on its banks.

A Week, ''Concord River''

A lake is the landscape's most beautiful and expressive feature. It is earth's eye; looking into which the beholder measures the depth of his own nature.

Walden, ''Ponds''

Walden Pond

It has been conjectured that when the hill shook these stones rolled down its side and became the present shore [of Walden]. It is very certain, at any rate, that once there was no pond here, and now there is one; and this Indian fable does not in any respect conflict with the account of that ancient settler whom I have mentioned, who remembers so well when he first came here with his divining-rod, saw a thin vapor rising from the sward, and the hazel pointed steadily downward, and he concluded to dig a well here. . . . If the name was not derived from that of some English locality,—Saffron Walden, for instance,—one might suppose that it was called originally *Walled-in* Pond.

Walden, "Ponds"

. . . of all the characters I have known, perhaps Walden wears best, and best preserves its purity. Many men have been likened to it, but few deserve that honor.

Walden, "Ponds"

. . . in September or October, Walden is a perfect forest mirror, set round with stones as precious to my eye as if fewer or rarer. Nothing so fair, so pure, and at the same time so large, as a lake, perchance, lies on the surface of the earth.

Walden, "Ponds"

The pure Walden water is mingled with the sacred water of the Ganges.

Walden, "Pond in Winter"

Trees

The tree is full of poetry.

Journal, July 16, 1852

It is the living spirit of the tree, not its spirit of turpentine, with which I sympathize, and which heals my cuts. It is as immortal as I am, and perchance will go to as high a heaven, there to tower above me still.

Maine Woods, ''Chesuncook''

It is worse than boorish, it is criminal, to inflict an unnecessary injury on the tree that feeds or shadows us. Old trees are our parents, and our parents' parents, perchance. If you would learn the secrets of Nature, you must practice more humanity than others. . . . Behold a man cutting down a tree to come at the fruit! What is the moral of such an act?

Journal, October 23, 1855

Nothing stands up more free from blame in this world than a pine tree.

Journal, December 20, 1851

Each pine is like a great green feather stuck in the ground.

Journal, November 30, 1851

The trees indeed have hearts. With a certain affection the sun seems to send its farewell ray far and level over the copses to them, and they silently receive it with gratitude, like a group of settlers with their children.

The pines impress me as human. A slight vaporous cloud floats high over them, while in the west the sun goes down apace behind glowing pines, and golden clouds like mountains skirt the horizon.

Journal, December 20, 1851

Next to the scarlet, methinks the white shrub oaks make, or have made, the most brilliant show at a distance on hillsides. The latter is not very bright, unless seen between you and the sun, but there its abundant inward color is apparent.

Journal, October 14, 1857

How beautiful, when a whole tree is like one great scarlet fruit full of ripe juices, every leaf, from lowest limb to topmost spire, all aglow, especially if you look toward the sun! What more remarkable object can there be in the landscape?

Excursions, ''Autumnal Tints''

Flowers, Weeds, and Fruits

. . . flowers as well as weeds follow in the footsteps of man.

Excursions, ''Winter Walk''

The *Convolvulus sepium,* bindweed; morning-glory is the best name. It always refreshes me to see it. . . . I associate it with holiest morning hours. It may preside

over my morning walks and thoughts. There is a flower
for every mood of the mind.

Journal, June 25, 1852

Under the influence of the light and warmth, the petals
[of the lily] elevate or expand themselves in the middle,
becoming more and more convex, till at last, being
released at their overlapping points, they spring open
and quickly spread themselves equally, revealing their
yellow stamens. How satisfactory is the fragrance of this
flower! It is the emblem of purity. It reminds me of a
young country maiden. It is just so simple and un-
proved.

Journal, August 5, 1858

May I mature as perfectly, root and branch, as the poke!
Its stems are more beautiful than most flowers. It is the
emblem of a successful life, a not premature death,—
whose death is an ornament to nature. . . . Here are berries enough to paint the western sky with and play the
Bacchanal if you will. What flutes its ensanguined stems
would make, to be used in the dance! It is a royal plant. I
could spend the evening of the year musing amid the
poke stems.

Journal, August 23, 1853

To my senses the dicksonia fern has the most wild and
primitive fragrance, quite unalloyed and untamable,
such as no human institutions give out,—the early
morning fragrance of the world, antediluvian, strength
and hope imparting. They who scent it can never faint.

It is ever a new and untried field where it grows, and only when we think original thoughts can we perceive it.

Journal, September 24, 1859

The flowers of the apple are perhaps the most beautiful of any tree's, so copious and so delicious to both sight and scent. The walker is frequently tempted to turn and linger near some more than usually handsome one, whose blossoms are two-thirds expanded. How superior it is in these respects to the pear, whose blossoms are neither colored nor fragrant!

Excursions, "Wild Apples"

. . . the apple emulates man's independence and enterprise.

Excursions, "Wild Apples"

From my experience with wild apples, I can understand that there may be reason for a savage's preferring many kinds of food which the civilized man rejects. The former has the palate of an outdoor man. It takes a savage or wild taste to appreciate wild fruit.

What a healthy out-of-door appetite it takes to relish the apple of life, the apple of the world, then.

Excursions, "Wild Apples"

It is a vulgar error to suppose that you have tasted huckleberries who never plucked them. . . . The ambrosial and essential part of the fruit is lost with the bloom which is rubbed off in the market cart, and they become mere provender.

Walden, "Ponds"

Animals

So far as our noblest hardwood forests are concerned, the animals, especially squirrels and jays, are our greatest and almost only benefactors. It is to them that we owe this gift. It is not in vain that the squirrels live in or about every forest tree, or hollow log, and every wall and heap of stones.

Journal, October 31, 1860

I spend a considerable portion of my time observing the habits of the wild animals, my brute neighbors. By their various movements and migrations they fetch the year about to me. Very significant are the flight of geese and the migration of suckers, etc., etc. But when I consider that the nobler animals have been exterminated here,— the cougar, panther, lynx, wolverene, wolf, bear, moose, deer, the beaver, the turkey, etc., etc.,—I cannot but feel as if I lived in a tamed, and, as it were, emasculated country. Would not the motions of those larger and wilder animals have been more significant still? Is it not a maimed and imperfect nature that I am conversant with? As if I were to study a tribe of Indians that had lost all its warriors. Do not the forest and meadow now lack expression, now that I never see nor think of the moose with a lesser forest on his head in the one, nor of the beaver in the other?

Journal, March 23, 1856

The bream, appreciated, floats in the pond as the centre of the system, another image of God. Its life no man can explain more than he can his own. I want you to perceive the mystery of the bream. I have a contemporary in Walden. It has fins where I have legs and arms. I have a friend among the fishes, at least a new acquaintance. Its character will interest me, I trust, not its clothes and anatomy. I do not want it to eat.

Journal, November 30, 1858

I think that the different epochs in the revolution of the seasons may perhaps be best marked by the notes of reptiles. They express, as it were, the very feelings of the earth or nature. They are perfect thermometers, hygrometers, and barometers.

Journal, May 6, 1858

I saw a snake by the roadside and touched him with my foot to see if he were alive. He had a toad in his jaws, which he was preparing to swallow with his jaws distended to three times his width, but he relinquished his prey in haste and fled; and I thought, as the toad jumped leisurely away with his slime-covered hind-quarters glistening in the sun, as if I, his deliverer, wished to interrupt his meditations,—without a shriek or fainting,—I thought what a healthy indifference he manifested. Is not this the broad earth still? he said.

Journal, August 23, 1851

Birds

The first sparrow of spring! The year beginning with younger hope than ever!

Walden, "Spring"

If you would have the song of the sparrow inspire you a thousand years hence, let your life be in harmony with its strain to-day.

Journal, May 12, 1857

As I come over the hill, I hear the wood thrush singing his evening lay. This is the only bird whose note affects me like music, affects the flow and tenor of my thought, my fancy and imagination. It lifts and exhilarates me. It is inspiring. It is a medicative draught to my soul. It is an elixir to my eyes and a fountain of youth to all my senses. It changes all hours to an eternal morning. It banishes all trivialness. It reinstates me in my dominion, makes me the lord of creation, is chief musician of my court. This minstral sings in a time, a heroic age, with which no event in the village can be contemporary.

Journal, June 22, 1853

The bluebird carries the sky on his back.

Journal, April 3, 1852

I was one evening passing a retired farmhouse which had a smooth green plat before it, just after sundown, when I saw a hen turkey which had gone to roost on the front fence with her wings outspread over her young now pretty well advanced, who were roosting on the next rail a foot or two below her. It completed a picture of rural repose and happiness such as I had not seen for a long time.

Journal, 1850, undated

The scream of the jay is a true winter sound. It is wholly without sentiment, and in harmony with winter.

Journal, February 2, 1854

The crow, flying high, touches the tympanum of the sky for us, and reveals the tone of it. What does it avail to look at a thermometer or barometer compared with listening to his note? He informs me that Nature is in the tenderest mood possible, and I hear the very flutterings of her heart.

Journal, January 30, 1860

When I hear a robin sing at sunset, I cannot help contrasting the equanimity of Nature with the bustle and impatience of man.

Journal, April 25, 1841

I rejoice that there are owls. Let them do the idiotic and maniacal hooting for men.

Walden, ''Sounds''

Time

All questions rely on the present for their solution. Time measures nothing but itself.

A Week, ''Thursday''

Time hides no treasures; we want not its *then*, but its *now*. We do not complain that the mountains in the horizon are blue and indistinct; they are the more like the heavens.

Journal, August 9, 1841

Time is but the stream I go a-fishing in. I drink at it; but while I drink I see the sandy bottom and detect how shallow it is. Its thin current slides away, but eternity remains.

Walden, ''Where I Lived''

I do not so much wish to know how to economize time as how to spend it, by what means to grow rich, that the day may not have been in vain.

Journal, September 7, 1851

I must live above all in the present.

Journal, January 7, 1851

Days

The day is an epitome of the year. The night is the winter, the morning and evening are the spring and fall, and the noon is the summer.

Walden, ''Spring''

Let us spend one day as deliberately as Nature, and not be thrown off the track by every nutshell and mosquito's wing that falls on the rails.

Walden, ''Where I Lived''

Morning

Morning is when I am awake and there is a dawn in me. . . . To be awake is to be alive. I have never yet met a man who was quite awake. How could I have looked him in the face?

Walden, "Where I Lived"

In the morning we do not believe in expediency; we will start afresh, and have no patching, no temporary fixtures. The afternoon man has an interest in the past; his eye is divided, and he sees indifferently well either way.

Journal, April 4, 1839

The morning, which is the most memorable season of the day, is the awakening hour. . . . All memorable events, I should say, transpire in morning time and in a morning atmosphere. The Vedas say, "All intelligences awake with the morning." Poetry and art, and the fairest and most memorable of the actions of men, date from such an hour.

Walden, "Where I Lived"

As we grow older, is it not ominous that we have more to write about evening, less about morning? We must associate more with the early hours.

Journal, February 24, 1852

Seasons

It is in vain to write on the seasons unless you have the seasons in you.

Journal, January 23, 1858

Spring is the reign of water; summer, of heat and dryness; winter, of cold.

Journal, July 24, 1853

As every season seems best to us in its turn, so the coming in of spring is like the creation of Cosmos out of Chaos and the realization of the Golden Age.

Walden, "Spring"

When the frogs dream, and the grass waves, and the buttercups toss their heads, and the heat disposes to bathe in the ponds and streams, then is summer begun.

Journal, June 8, 1850

Our Indian summer, I am tempted to say, is the finest season of the year. Here has been such a day as I think Italy never sees.

Journal, October 31, 1850

Live in each season as it passes; breathe the air, drink the drink, taste the fruit, and resign yourself to the influences of each. . . . Be blown on by all the winds. Open all your pores and bathe in all the tides of Nature, in all her streams and oceans, at all seasons. . . . Grow green with spring, yellow and ripe with autumn. Drink of each

season's influence as a vial, a true panacea of all
remedies mixed for your especial use.

Journal, August 23, 1853

The autumnal change of our woods has not made a deep
impression on our own literature yet. October has
hardly tinged our poetry.

Excursions, ''Autumnal Tints''

October is the month of painted leaves, of ripe leaves,
when all the earth, not merely flowers, but fruits and
leaves, are ripe. With respect to its colors and its season,
it is the sunset month of the year, when the earth is
painted like the sunset sky. This rich glow flashes round
the world. This light fades into the clear, white, leafless
twilight of November, and whatever more glowing sunset or Indian summer we have then is the afterglow of
the year. In October the man is ripe even to his stalk and
leaves; he is pervaded by his genius, when all the forest
is a universal harvest, whether he possesses the enduring color of the pines, which it takes two years to ripen
and wither, or the brilliant color of the deciduous trees,
which fade the first fall.

Journal, November 14, 1853

In winter we lead a more inward life. Our hearts are
warm and cheery, like cottages under drifts, whose win-
dows and doors are half concealed, but from whose
chimneys the smoke cheerfully ascends.

Excursions, ''Winter Walk''

To us snow and cold seem a mere delaying of the spring. How far we are from understanding the value of these things in the economy of Nature!

Journal, March 8, 1859

The finest winter day is a cold but clear and glittering one. There is a remarkable life in the air then, and birds and other creatures appear to feel it, to be excited and invigorated by it.

Journal, January 25, 1860

Sounds and Silence

Any melodious sound apprises me of the infinite wealth of God.

Consciousness in Concord

Nature makes no noise. The howling storm, the rustling leaf, the pattering rain are no disturbance, there is an essential and unexplored harmony in them.

Journal, November 18, 1837

Certainly the voice of no bird or beast can be compared with that of man for true melody. All other sounds seem to be hushed, as if their possessors were attending, when the voice of man is heard in melody. . . . The bird's song is a mere interjectional shout of joy; man's a glorious expression of the foundations of his joy.

Journal, September 8, 1851

The sound of the crickets at dawn after these first sultry nights seems like the dreaming of the earth still continued into the daylight. I love that early twilight hour when the crickets still creak right on with such dewy faith and promise, as if it were still night,—expressing the innocence of morning,—when the creak of the cricket is fresh and bedewed. While the creak of the cricket has that ambrosial sound, no crime can be committed. It buries Greece and home past resurrection. The earth-song of the cricket! Before Christianity was, it is.

Journal, June 17, 1852

When I listen to the faint creaking of the crickets, it seems as if my course for the future lay that way.

Consciousness in Concord

As the truest society approaches always nearer to solitude, so the most excellent speech finally falls into Silence. Silence is audible to all men, at all times, and in all places.

A Week, "Friday"

Silence alone is worthy to be heard. Silence is of a various depth and fertility, like soil. Now it is a mere Sahara, where men perish of hunger and thirst, now a fertile bottom, or prairie, of the West. As I leave the village, drawing nearer to the woods, I listen from time to time to hear the hounds of Silence baying the Moon,—to know if they are on the track of any game. If there's no Diana in the night, what is it worth? I hark the goddess Diana. The silence rings; it is musical and thrills me. A night in which the silence was audible. I hear the unspeakable.

Journal, January 21, 1853

Beauty

Beauty is where it is perceived. When I see the sun shining on the woods across the pond, I think this side the richer which sees it.

Consciousness in Concord

The perception of beauty is a moral test.

Journal, June 21, 1852

Always the line of beauty is a curve.

Reform Papers, "The Service"

For beauty, give me trees with the fur on.

Maine Woods, "Chesuncook"

Colors

We love to see any part of the earth tinged with blue, cerulean, the color of the sky, the celestial color.

Journal, May 25, 1851

How transitory the perfect beauty of the rose and lily! The highest, intensest color belongs to the land, the purest, perchance, to the water.

Journal, June 26, 1852

In certain lights, as yesterday against the snow, nothing can be more splendid and celestial than the color of the bluebird.

Journal, April 19, 1854

The rose owes its preeminence in great measure to its color. It is said to be from the Celtic *rhos,* red. It is nature's most precious color.

Journal, July 11, 1852

Green is essentially *vivid,* or the color of life, and it is therefore most brilliant when a plant is moist or most alive.

Journal, April 2, 1855

Brown is the color for me, the color of our coats and our daily lives, the color of the poor man's loaf.

Journal, March 28, 1859

It is surprising what a variety of distinct colors the winter can show us, using but few pigments, so to call them. The principal charm of a winter walk over ice is perhaps the peculiar and pure colors exhibited.

There is the *red* of the sunset sky, and of the snow at evening, and in rainbow flocks during the day, and in sundogs.

The *blue* of the sky, and of the ice and water reflected, and of shadows on snow.

The *yellow* of the sun and the morning and evening sky, and of the sedge (or straw-color, bright when lit on edge of ice at evening), and *all three* in hoar frost crystals.

Then, for the secondary, there is the *purple* of the snow in drifts or on hills, of the mountains, and clouds at evening.

The *green* of evergreen woods, of the sky, and of the ice and water toward evening.

The *orange* of the sky at evening.

The *white* of snow and clouds, and the *black* of clouds, of water agitated, and water saturating thin snow on ice.

The *russet* and *brown* and *gray,* etc., of deciduous woods.

The *tawny* of the bare earth.

Journal, February 13, 1860

Walking

It is a great art to saunter.

Journal, April 26, 1841

An early morning walk is a blessing for the whole day.

Journal, April 20, 1840

Many men walk by day; few walk by night. It is a very different season.

Excursions, ''Night and Moonlight''

I think that I cannot preserve my health and spirits, unless I spend four hours a day at least—and it is commonly more than that—sauntering through the woods and over the hills and fields, absolutely free from all worldly engagements.

Excursions, ''Walking''

I have met with but one or two persons in the course of my life who understood the art of Walking, that is, of taking walks,—who had a genius, so to speak, for *sauntering,* which word is beautifully derived "from idle people who roved about the country, in the Middle Ages, and asked charity, under pretense of going *a la Sainte Terre,*" to the Holy Land, till the children exclaimed, "There goes a *Sainte-Terrer,*" a Saunterer, a Holy-Lander. They who never go to the Holy Land in their walks, as they pretend, are indeed mere idlers and vagabonds; but they who do go there are saunterers in the good sense, such as I mean. . . . For every walk is a sort of crusade, preached by some Peter the Hermit in us, to go forth and reconquer this Holy Land from the hands of the Infidels.

Excursions, "Walking"

We should go forth on the shortest walk, perchance, in the spirit of undying adventure, never to return,—prepared to send back our imbalmed hearts only as relics to our desolate kingdoms. If you are ready to leave father and mother, and brother and sister, and wife and child and friends, and never see them again,—if you have paid your debts, and made your will, and settled all your affairs, and are a free man, then you are ready for a walk.

Excursions, "Walking"

The Indian

Wherever I go, I tread in the tracks of the Indian.

Journal, March 19, 1842

The Indian, who can find his way so wonderfully in the woods, possesses so much intelligence which the white man does not,—and it increases my own capacity, as well as faith, to observe it. I rejoice to find that intelligence flows in other channels than I knew. It redeems for me portions of what seemed brutish before.

Correspondence, To H. G. O. Blake,
August 18, 1857

Nature must have made a thousand revelations to them [the Indians] which are still secrets to us.

Maine Woods, "Allegash"

I have much to learn of the Indian, nothing of the missionary.

Maine Woods, "Allegash"

The constitution of the Indian mind appears to be the very opposite to that of the white man. He is acquainted with a different side of nature. He measures his life by winters, not summers. His year is not measured by the sun, but consists of a certain number of moons, and his moons are measured not by days, but by nights. He has taken hold of the dark side of nature; the white man, the bright side.

Journal, October 25, 1852

The charm of the Indian to me is that he stands free and unconstrained in Nature, is her inhabitant and not her guest, and wears her easily and gracefully. But the civilized man has the habits of the house. His house is a prison, in which he finds himself oppressed and confined, not sheltered and protected.

Journal, April 26, 1841

The savage may be, and often is a sage. Our Indian is more of a man than the inhabitant of a city. He lives as a man, he thinks as a man, he dies as a man.

Sanborn, ''College Essays,''
quoted in Life of Thoreau

KNOWLEDGE AND IGNORANCE

The intellect is a cleaver; it discerns and rifts its way into the secret of things.

Walden, ''Where I Lived''

There is a chasm between knowledge and ignorance which the arches of science can never span.

A Week, ''Sunday''

My desire for knowledge is intermittent, but my desire to bathe my head in atmospheres unknown to my feet is perennial and constant. The highest that we can attain to is not Knowledge, but Sympathy with Intelligence.

Excursions, ''Walking''

Knowledge does not come to us by details, but in flashes of light from heaven.

Miscellanies, ''Life Without Principle''

The universe is wider than our views of it.

Walden, ''Conclusion''

It is only when we forget all our learning that we begin to know. I do not get nearer by a hair's breadth to any natural object so long as I presume that I have an introduction to it from some learned man. To conceive of

it with a total apprehension I must for the thousandth
time approach it as something totally strange.

Journal, October 4, 1859

Our Golden Age must after all be a pastoral one, we
would be simple men in ignorance, and not accom-
plished in wisdom. . . . Let us grow to the full stature of
our humbleness—ere we aspire to be greater.

Consciousness in Concord

Facts

Let us not underrate the value of a fact; it will one day
flower in a truth.

Excursions, ''Natural History of Massachusetts''

I have a commonplace-book for facts and another for
poetry, but I find it difficult always to preserve the vague
distinction which I had in my mind, for the most interesting and beautiful facts are so much the more
poetry and that is their success. They are *translated*
from earth to heaven. I see that if my facts were suffi-
ciently vital and significant,—perhaps transmuted more
into the substance of the human mind,—I should need
but one book of poetry to contain them all.

Journal, February 18, 1852

A fact stated barely is dry. It must be the vehicle of some
humanity in order to interest us. It is like giving a man a
stone when he asks you for bread. Ultimately the moral
is all in all, and we do not mind it if inferior truth is

sacrificed to superior, as when the moralist fables and makes animals speak and act like men. It must be warm, moist, incarnated,—have been breathed on at least. A man has not seen a thing who has not felt it.

Journal, February 23, 1860

I, too, would fain set down something beside facts. Facts should only be as the frame to my pictures; they should be material to the mythology which I am writing; not facts to assist men to make money, farmers to farm profitably, in any common sense; facts to tell who I am, and where I have been or what I have thought . . . My facts shall be falsehoods to the common sense. I would so state facts that they shall be significant, shall be myths or mythologic. Facts which the mind perceived, thoughts which the body thought,—with these I deal.

Journal, November 9, 1851

The most glorious fact in my experience is not anything that I have done or may hope to do, but a transient thought, or vision, or dream, which I have had. I would give all the wealth of the world, and all the deeds of all the heroes, for one true vision.

A Week, "Monday"

Wisdom

All wisdom is the reward of a discipline, conscious or unconscious.

Journal, September 5, 1851

I am sane only when I have risen above my common sense, when I do not take the foolish view of things which is commonly taken, when I do not live for the low ends for which men commonly live. Wisdom is not common.

Journal, June 22, 1851

A man is wise with the wisdom of his time only, and ignorant with its ignorance. Observe how the greatest minds yield in some degree to the superstitions of their age.

Journal, January 31, 1853

Wisdom does not inspect, but behold. We must look a long time before we can see.

Excursions, "Natural History of Massachusetts"

Give me a sentence which no intelligence can understand. There must be a kind of life and palpitation to it, and under its words a kind of blood must circulate forever.

A Week, "Monday"

Thought

The best thought is not only without sombreness, but even without morality.

Journal, August 1, 1841

We are accustomed to say in New England that few and fewer pigeons visit us every year. Our forests furnish no mast for them. So, it would seem few and fewer thoughts visit each growing man from year to year, for the grove in our minds is laid waste,—sold to feed unnecessary fires of ambition, or send to mill,—and there is scarcely a twig left for them to perch on. . . . Our winged thoughts are turned to poultry. They no longer soar . . .

Excursions, ''Walking''

You come from attending the funeral of mankind to attend to a natural phenomenon. A little thought is sexton to all the world.

Miscellanies, ''Life Without Principle''

Conscience

No man ever stood the lower in my estimation for having a patch in his clothes; yet I am sure that there is a greater anxiety, commonly, to have fashionable, or at least clean and unpatched clothes, than to have a sound conscience.

Walden, ''Economy''

Philosophy

Say, Not so, and you will outcircle the philosophers.

Journal, June 26, 1840

There are nowadays professors of philosophy, but not philosophers. Yet it is admirable to profess because it was once admirable to live. To be a philosopher is not merely to have subtle thoughts, nor even to found a school, but so to love wisdom as to live according to its dictates, a life of simplicity, independence, magnanimity, and trust. It is to solve some of the problems of life, not only theoretically, but practically.

Walden, "Economy"

The philosopher's conception of things will, above all, be truer than other men's, and his philosophy will subordinate all the circumstances of life. To live like a philosopher is to live, not foolishly, like other men, but wisely and according to universal laws.

Miscellanies, "Carlyle and His Works"

In comparison with the philosophers of the East, we may say that modern Europe has yet given birth to none. Beside the vast and cosmogonal philosophy of the Bhagvat-Geeta, even our Shakespeare seems sometimes youthfully green and practical merely.

A Week, "Monday"

Genius

No man ever followed his genius till it misled him.

Walden, "Higher Laws"

Show me a man who consults his genius, and you have shown me a man who cannot be advised. . . . And he alone knows when something comes between him and his object.

Journal, December 27, 1858

The Man of Genius may at the same time be, indeed is commonly, an Artist, but the two are not to be confounded. The Man of Genius, referred to mankind, is an originator, an inspired or demonic man, who produces a perfect work in obedience to laws yet unexplored. The artist is he who detects and applies the law from observation of the works of Genius, whether of man or nature. The Artisan is he who merely applies the rules which others have detected. There has been no man of pure Genius, as there has been none wholly destitute of Genius.

A Week, "Thursday"

The musty records of history, like the catacombs, contain the perishable remains, but only in the breast of genius are embalmed the souls of heroes.

Miscellanies, "Carlyle and His Works"

Education

The end of life is education. An education is good or bad according to the disposition or frame of mind it induces.

Sanborn, "College Essays," quoted in *Life of Thoreau*

What does education often do? It makes a straight-cut ditch of a free, meandering brook.

Journal, 1850, undated

I would make education a pleasant thing both to the teacher and the scholar. This discipline, which we allow to be the end of life, should not be one thing in the schoolroom, and another in the street. We should seek to be fellow students with the pupil, and we should learn of, as well as with him, if we would be most helpful to him.

Correspondence, To Orestes Brownson,
December 30, 1837

I remember how glad I was when I was kept from school a half a day to pick huckleberries on a neighboring hill all by myself to make a pudding for the family dinner. Ah, they got nothing but the pudding, but I got invaluable experience beside! A half a day of liberty like that was like the promise of life eternal. It was emancipation in New England. O, what a day was there, my countrymen!

Journal, July 16, 1851

It would really be no small advantage if every college were thus located at the base of a mountain, as good at least as one well-endowed professorship. It were as well to be educated in the shadow of a mountain as in more classical shades. Some will remember, no doubt, not only that they went to the college, but that they went to the mountain. Every visit to its summit would, as it were, generalize the particular information gained below, and subject it to more catholic tests.

A Week, ''Tuesday''

When I read some of the rules for speaking and writing the English language correctly,—as that a sentence must never end with a particle,—and perceive how implicitly even the learned obey it, I think—

> Any fool can make a rule
> And every fool will mind it.

Journal, February 3, 1860

It is impossible to give the soldier a good education without making him a deserter. His natural foe is the government that drills him. What would any philanthropist who felt an interest in these men's welfare naturally do, but first of all teach them so to respect themselves that they could not be hired for this work, whatever might be the consequences to this government or that?—not drill a few, but educate all.

A Yankee in Canada, ''Quebec and Montmorenci''

History

Ancient history has an air of antiquity. It should be more modern. It is written as if the spectator should be thinking of the backside of the picture on the wall, or as if the author expected that the dead would be his readers, and wished to detail to them their own experience.

A Week, ''Monday''

History has neither the venerableness of antiquity, nor the freshness of the modern. . . . It has been so written, for the most part, that the times it describes are with remarkable propriety called *dark ages.* They are dark, as one has observed, because we are so in the dark about them. The sun rarely shines in history, what with the dust and confusion; and when we meet with any cheering fact which implies the presence of this luminary, we excerpt and modernize it.

A Week, "Monday"

ART

The highest condition of art is artlessness.
Journal, June 26, 1840

To affect the quality of the day, that is the highest of arts.
Walden, ''Where I Lived''

. . . any surpassing work of art is strange and wild to the mass of men, as is genius itself.
Journal, February 16, 1859

Art can never match the luxury and superfluity of Nature. In the former all is seen; it cannot afford concealed wealth, and is niggardly in comparison; but Nature, even when she is scant and thin outwardly, satisfies us still by the assurance of a certain generosity at the roots.
A Week, ''Thursday''

Art is not tame, and Nature is not wild, in the ordinary sense. A perfect work of man's art would also be wild or natural in a good sense. Man tames Nature only that he may at last make her more free even than he found her, though he may never yet have succeeded.
A Week, ''Thursday''

Music

It is remarkable that our institutions can stand before music, it is so revolutionary.

Journal, October 17, 1857

How cultivated, how sweet and glorious, is music! Men have brought this art to great perfection, the art of modulating sound, by long practice since the world began. What superiority over the rude harmony of savages! There is something glorious and flower-like in it. What a contrast this evening melody with the occupations of the day! It is perhaps the most admirable accomplishment of man.

Journal, June 18, 1852

The music of all creatures has to do with their loves, even of toads and frogs. Is it not the same with man?

Journal, May 6, 1852

When I hear a strain of music from across the street, I put away Homer and Shakespeare, and read them in the original.

Consciousness in Concord

In a world of peace and love music would be the universal language, and men greet each other in the fields in such accents, as a Beethoven now utters at rare intervals from a distance. All things obey music as they obey virtue. It is the herald of virtue. It is God's voice.

Reform Papers, ''The Service''

One will lose no music by not attending the oratorios and operas. The really inspiring melodies are cheap and universal, and are as audible to the poor man's son as to the rich man's.

Journal, August 8, 1851

On the railroad I hear the telegraph. This is the lyre that is as old as the world. I put my ear to the post, and the sound seems to be in the core of the post, directly against my ear. This is all of music. The utmost refinements of art, methinks, can go no further.

Journal, March 29, 1853

Poetry

Poetry is the mysticism of mankind. . . . It is only by a miracle that poetry is written at all. It is not a recoverable thought, but a hue caught from a vaster receding thought.

A Week, ''Thursday''

Poetry *implies* the whole truth. Philosophy *expresses* a particle of it.

Journal, January 26, 1852

. . . the divinest poem, or the life of a great man, is the severest satire; as impersonal as Nature herself, and like the sighs of her winds in the woods, which convey ever a slight reproof to the hearer.

A Week, ''Thursday''

There is no doubt that the loftiest written wisdom is either rhymed or in some way musically measured,—is, in form as well as substance, poetry; ... Yet poetry, though the last and finest result, is a natural fruit. As naturally as the oak bears an acorn, and the vine a gourd, man bears a poem, either spoken or done.

A Week, ''Sunday''

I do not know of any poetry to quote which adequately expresses this yearning for the Wild. Approached from this side, the best poetry is tame. I do not know where to find in any literature, ancient or modern, any account which contents me of that Nature with which even I am acquainted. . . . Mythology comes nearer to it than anything.

Excursions, ''Walking''

The Poet

The works of the great poets have never yet been read by mankind, for only great poets can read them.

Walden, ''Reading''

The true poet will ever live aloof from society, wild to it, as the finest singer is the wood thrush, a forest bird.

Journal, May 11, 1854

It is not important that the poet should say some particular thing, but should speak in harmony with nature. The tone and pitch of his voice is the main thing.

Journal, April 2, 1858

There are two classes of men called poets. The one cultivates life, the other art,—one seeks food for nutriment, the other for flavor; one satisfies hunger, the other gratifies the palate. There are two kinds of writing, both great and rare,—one that of genius, or the inspired, the other of intellect and taste, in the intervals of inspiration. The former is above criticism, always correct, giving the law to criticism. It vibrates and pulsates with life forever. It is sacred, and to be read with reverence, as the works of nature are studied.

A Week, ''Friday''

That reader who most fully appreciates the poet, and derives the greatest pleasure from his works, himself lives in circumstances most like those of the poet himself.

Journal, January 28, 1852

The one who came from farthest to my lodge, through deepest snows and most dismal tempests, was a poet. A farmer, a hunter, a soldier, a reporter, even a philosopher, may be daunted; but nothing can deter a poet, for he is actuated by pure love.

Walden, ''Former Inhabitants''

. . . Chaucer's is the first name after that misty weather in which Ossian lived, which can detain us long. Indeed, though he represents so different a culture and society, he may be regarded as in many respects the Homer of the English poets. Perhaps he is the youthfulest of them all. We return to him as to the purest well, the fountain farthest removed from the highway of desultory life. He is so natural and cheerful, compared with later poets, that we might almost regard him as a personification of spring.

A Week, "Friday"

The prosaic man sees things baldly, or with the bodily sense; but the poet sees them clad in beauty, with the spiritual sense.

Journal, December 9, 1859

The poet is he who can write some pure mythology today without the aid of posterity.

A Week, "Sunday"

The Writer

He is not the great writer, who is afraid to let the world know that he ever committed an impropriety. Does it not know that all men are mortal?

Journal, 1845-47, undated

A writer who does not speak out of a full experience uses torpid words, wooden or lifeless words, such words as "humanitary," which have a paralysis in their tails.

Journal, July 14, 1852

If thou art a writer, write as if thy time were short, for it is indeed short at the longest. Improve each occasion when thy soul is reached. Drain the cup of inspiration to its last dregs. . . . The spring will not last forever. These fertile and expanding seasons of thy life, when the rain reaches thy root, when thy vigor shoots, when thy flower is budding, shall be fewer and farther between. Again I say, Remember thy Creator in the days of thy youth. Use and commit to life what you cannot commit to memory.

Journal, January 24, 1852

The writer must direct his sentences as carefully and leisurely as the marksman his rifle, who shoots sitting and with a rest, with patent sights and conical balls beside. He must not merely seem to speak the truth. He must really speak it. If you foresee that a part of your essay will topple down after the lapse of time, throw it down now yourself.

Journal, January 26, 1852

Reading

I did not read books the first summer [at Walden]; I hoed beans. Nay, I often did better than this.

Walden, ''Sounds''

I read one or two shallow books of travel in the intervals of my work, till that employment made me ashamed of myself, and I asked where it was then that *I* lived.

Walden, ''Reading''

Read not the Times. Read the Eternities.

Miscellanies, ''Life Without Principle''

To read well, that is, to read true books in a true spirit, is a noble exercise, and one that will task the reader more than any exercise which the customs of the day esteem.

Walden, "Reading"

It would be worth the while to select our reading, for books are the society we keep; . . . Read the best books first, or you may not have a chance to read them at all.

A Week, "Sunday"

Reading the classics or conversing with those old Greeks and Latins in their surviving works, is like walking amid the stars and constellations, a high and by way serene to travel.

A Week, "Tuesday"

I never read a novel, they have so little real life and thought in them. The reading which I love best is the scriptures of the several nations, though it happens that I am better acquainted with those of the Hindoos, the Chinese, and the Persians, than of the Hebrews, which I have come to last. Give me one of these bibles, and you have silenced me for a while.

A Week, "Sunday"

Writing

By the quality of a man's writing, by the elevation of its tone, you may measure his self-respect. How shall a man continue his culture after manhood?

Journal, September 5, 1851

A written word is the choicest of relics. It is something at once more intimate with us and more universal than any other work of art. It is the work of art nearest to life itself.

Walden, "Reading"

Do nothing merely out of good resolutions. Discipline yourself only to yield to love; suffer yourself to be attracted. It is in vain to write on chosen themes. We must wait till they have kindled a flame in our minds. There must be the copulating and generating force of love behind every effort destined to be successful. The cold resolve gives birth to, begets, nothing. The theme that seeks me, not I it. The poet's relation to his theme is the relation of lovers. It is no more to be courted. Obey, report.

Journal, January 30, 1852

Write while the heat is in you. When the farmer burns a hole in his yoke, he carries the hot iron quickly from the fire to the wood, for every moment it is less effectual to penetrate (pierce) it. It must be used instantly, or it is useless. The writer who postpones the recording of his thoughts uses an iron which has cooled to burn a hole with. He cannot inflame the minds of his audience.

Journal, February 10, 1852

Every sentence should contain some twilight or night. At least the light in it should be the yellow or creamy light of the moon or the fine beams of stars, and not the white light of day. The peculiar dusky serenity of the sentences must not allow the reader to forget that it is evening or night, without my saying that it is dark. Otherwise he will, of course, presume a daylight atmosphere.

Journal, June 26, 1852

You must try a thousand themes before you find the right one, as nature makes a thousand acorns to get one oak. He is a wise man and experienced who has taken many views; to whom stones and plants and animals and a myriad objects have each suggested something, contributed something.

Journal, September 4, 1851

Though I write every day, yet when I say a good thing it seems as if I wrote but rarely.

Journal, February 26, 1841

Who cares what a man's style is, so [long as] it is intelligible,—as intelligible as his thought. Literally and really, the style is no more than the *stylus,* the pen he writes with; and it is not worth scraping and polishing, and gilding, unless it will write his thoughts the better for it. It is something for use, and not to look at.

Miscellanies, ''Carlyle and His Works''

It is the fault of some excellent writers . . . that they express themselves with too great fullness and detail. They give the most faithful, natural, and lifelike account of their sensations, mental and physical, but they lack moderation and sententiousness. They do not affect us by an ineffectual earnestness and a reserve of meaning, like a stutterer; they say all they mean. Their sentences are not concentrated and nutty. Sentences which suggest far more than they say, which have an atmosphere about them, which do not merely report an old, but make a new, impression; sentences which suggest as many things and are as durable as a Roman aqueduct; to frame these, that is the *art* of writing.

Journal, August 22, 1851

I find that I can criticise my composition best when I stand at a little distance from it,—when I do not see it, for instance. I make a little chapter of contents which enables me to recall it page by page to my mind, and judge it more impartially when my manuscript is out of the way. The distraction of surveying enables me rapidly to take new points of view. A day or two surveying is equal to a journey.

Journal, April 8, 1854

Journal

"What are you doing now?" he [Emerson?] asked. "Do you keep a journal?" So I make my first entry today.

Journal, October 22, 1837

My Journal is that of me which would else spill over and run to waste, gleanings from the field which in action I reap. I must not live for it, but in it for the gods.

Journal, February 8, 1841

"Says I to myself" should be the motto of my journal.

Journal, November 11, 1851

A journal, [is] a book that shall contain a record of all your joy, your ecstasy.

Journal, July 13, 1852

A journal is a record of experiences and growth, not a preserve of things well done or said. I am occasionally reminded of a statement which I have made in conversation and immediately forgotten, which would read much better than what I put in my journal. It is a ripe, dry fruit of long-past experience which falls from me easily, without giving pain or pleasure. The charm of the journal must consist in a certain greenness, though freshness, and not in maturity. Here I cannot afford to be remembering what I said or did my scurf cast off, but what I am and aspire to become.

Journal, January 24, 1856

I would fain make two reports in my Journal, first the incidents and observations of to-day; and by to-morrow I review the same and record what was omitted before, which will often be the most significant and poetic part. I do not know at first what it is that charms me. The men and things of to-day are wont to lie fairer and truer in to-morrow's memory.

Journal, March 27, 1857

Books

Much is published, but little printed.

Walden, "Sounds"

An honest book's the noblest work of Man.

Correspondence, To Helen Thoreau,
January 21, 1840

Books of natural history make the most cheerful winter reading.

Excursions, "Natural History of Massachusetts"

There are few books which are fit to be remembered in our wisest hours, but the Iliad is brightest in the serenest days, and embodies still all the sunlight that fell on Asia Minor.

A Week, "Sunday"

RELIGION

What is religion? That which is never spoken.

Journal, August 18, 1858

In religion there is no society.

Journal, September 14, 1841

For my part if I have any creed it is so to live as to preserve and increase the susceptibleness of my nature to noble impulses—first to observe if any light shine on me, and then faithfully to follow it.

Correspondence, To Isaiah T. Williams,
September 8, 1841

A man's real faith is never contained in his creed, nor is his creed an article of his faith. The last is never adopted.

A Week, "Sunday"

Our religion is where our love is.

Correspondence, To Isaiah T. Williams,
September 8, 1841

Some years ago, the State met me in behalf of the Church, and commanded me to pay a certain sum toward the support of a clergyman whose preaching my father attended, but never I myself. "Pay," it said, "or be locked up in the jail." I declined to pay. But, unfortunately, another man saw fit to pay it. I did not see why the schoolmaster should be taxed to support the priest, and not the priest the schoolmaster; for I was not the State's schoolmaster, but I supported myself by voluntary subscription. . . . However, at the request of the selectmen, I condescended to make some such statement as this in writing:—''Know all men by these presents, that I, Henry Thoreau, do not wish to be regarded as a member of any incorporated society which I have not joined.'' This I gave to the town clerk; and he has it. The State, having thus learned that I did not wish to be regarded as a member of that church, has never made a like demand on me since; though it said that it must adhere to its original presumption that time. If I had known how to name them, I should then have signed off in detail from all the societies which I never signed on to; but I did not know where to find a complete list.

Miscellanies, ''Civil Disobedience''

I perceive no triumphant superiority in the so-called Christian over the so-called Mahometan. That nation is not Christian where the principles of humanity do not prevail, but the prejudices of race.

Journal, September 25, 1851

Christ was a sublime actor on the stage of the world. . . . Yet he taught mankind but imperfectly how to live; his thoughts were all directed toward another world. There is another kind of success than his. Even here we have a sort of living to get, and must buffet it somewhat longer. There are various tough problems yet to solve, and we must make shift to live, betwixt spirit and matter, such a human life as we can.

A Week, ''Sunday''

God

As I stand over the insect crawling amid the pine
needles on the forest floor, and endeavoring to conceal
itself from my sight, and ask myself why it will cherish
those humble thoughts, and hide its head from me who
might, perhaps, be its benefactor, and impart to its race
some cheering information, I am reminded of the greater
Benefactor and Intelligence that stands over me the
human insect.

Walden, ''Conclusion''

Remember thy Creator in the days of thy youth; *i.e.,* lay
up a store of natural influences. Sing while you may,
before the evil days come. He that hath ears, let him
hear. See, hear, smell, taste, etc., while these senses are
fresh and pure.

Journal, July 21, 1851

In eternity there is indeed something true and sublime.
But all these times and places and occasions are now and
here. God himself culminates in the present moment,
and will never be more divine in the lapse of all the ages.
And we are enabled to apprehend at all what is sublime
and noble only by the perpetual instilling and drenching
of the reality that surrounds us.

Walden, ''Where I Lived''

We can only live healthily the life the gods assign us. I
must receive my life as passively as the willow leaf that
flutters over the brook. I must not be for myself, but

God's work, and that is always good. I will wait the breezes patiently, and grow as Nature shall determine. My fate cannot but be grand so. We may live the life of a plant or an animal, without living an animal life. This constant and universal content of the animal comes of resting quietly in God's palm. I feel as if [I]* could at any time resign my life and the responsibility of living into God's hands, and become as innocent, free from care, as a plant or stone.

Journal, March 11, 1842

It seems to me that the god that is commonly worshipped in civilized countries is not at all divine, though he bears a divine name, but is the overwhelming authority and respectability of mankind combined. Men reverence one another, not yet God.

A Week, "Sunday"

In my Pantheon, Pan still reigns in his pristine glory, with his ruddy face, his flowing beard, and his shaggy body, his pipe and his crook, his nymph Echo, and his chosen daughter, Iambe; for the great god Pan is not dead, as was rumored. Perhaps of all the gods of New England and of ancient Greece, I am most constant at his shrine.

A Week, "Sunday"

Let God alone if need be. Methinks, if I loved him more, I should keep him,—I should keep myself rather,—at a

---

* Brackets appear in the original.

more respectful distance. It is not when I am going to meet him, but when I am just turning away and leaving him alone, that I discover that God is. I say, God. I am not sure that that is the name.

Correspondence, To H. G. O. Blake,
April 3, 1850

God cannot give us any other than self help.
Consciousness in Concord

Scriptures

The best scripture, after all, records but a meagre faith.
Excursions, "Winter Walk"

After time has sifted the literature of a people, there is left only their SCRIPTURE, for that is WRITING, *par excellence.* This is as true of the poets, as of the philosophers and moralists by profession; for what subsides in any of these is the moral only, to reappear as dry land at some remote epoch.
Miscellanies, "Carlyle and His Works"

I know of no book that has so few readers. There is none so truly strange, and heretical, and unpopular. To Christians, no less than Greeks and Jews, it is foolishness and a stumbling-block. There are, indeed, severe things in it which no man should read aloud more than once. "Seek first the kingdom of heaven." "Lay not up for yourselves treasures on earth." "If thou wilt be perfect, go and sell that thou hast, and give to the poor, and thou shalt have treasure in heaven." "For what is a man profited, if he shall gain the whole world, and lose his own soul? Or what shall a man give in exchange for his soul?" Think of this, Yankees! "Verily, I say unto you, if ye have faith as a grain of mustard seed, ye shall say unto this mountain, Remove hence to yonder place, and it shall remove; and nothing shall be impossible unto you." Think of repeating these things to a New England audience! thirdly, fourthly, fifteenthly, till there are three barrels of sermons! who, without cant, can read them aloud? Who, without cant, can hear them, and not go out of the meeting-house? They never *were* read, they never *were* heard. Let but one of these sentences be rightly read, from any pulpit in the land, and there would not be left one stone of that meeting-house upon another.

A Week, "Sunday"

The New Testament is remarkable for its pure morality; the best of the Hindoo Scripture, for its pure intellectuality. The reader is nowhere raised into and sustained in a higher, purer, or *rarer* region of thought than in the Bhagvat-Geeta.

A Week, "Monday"

In the morning I bathe my intellect in the stupendous and cosmogonal philosophy of the Bhagvat-Geeta, since whose composition years of the gods have elapsed, and in comparison with which our modern world and its literature seem puny and trivial; and I doubt if that philosophy is not to be referred to a previous state of existence, so remote is its sublimity from our conceptions.

Walden, ''Pond in Winter''

It would be worthy of the age to print together the collected Scriptures or Sacred Writings of the several nations, the Chinese, the Hindoos, the Persians, the Hebrews, and others, as the Scripture of mankind. . . . This is a work which Time will surely edit, reserved to crown the labors of the printing-press. This would be the Bible, or Book of Books, which let the missionaries carry to the uttermost parts of the earth.

A Week, ''Monday''

Spiritual Purity

All sensuality is one, though it takes many forms; all purity is one. It is the same whether a man eat, or drink, or cohabit, or sleep sensually. They are but one appetite, and we only need to see a person do any one of these things to know how great a sensualist he is. The impure can neither stand nor sit with purity.

Walden, ''Higher Laws''

How prompt we are to satisfy the hunger & thirst of our bodies; how slow to satisfy the hunger & thirst of our *souls.*

Correspondence, To H. G. O. Blake,
February 27, 1853

For every inferior, earthly pleasure we forego, a superior, celestial one is substituted.

Journal, 1837-47, undated

Chastity is the flowering of man; and what are called Genius, Heroism, Holiness, and the like, are but various fruits which succeed it.

Walden, ''Higher Laws''

Every man is the builder of a temple, called his body, to the god he worships, after a style purely his own, nor can he get off by hammering marble instead. We are all sculptors and painters, and our material is our own flesh and blood and bones.

Walden, ''Higher Laws''

Virtue

Man's moral nature is a riddle which only eternity can solve.

Journal, March 19, 1842

We cannot well do without our sins; they are the highway of our virtue.

Journal, March 22, 1842

Our whole life is startlingly moral. There is never an instant's truce between virtue and vice. Goodness is the only investment that never fails.

Walden, ''Higher Laws''

The broadest and most prevalent error requires the most disinterested virtue to sustain it.

Miscellanies, "Civil Disobedience"

Nature is hard to be overcome, but she must be overcome.

Walden, "Higher Laws"

Absolutely speaking, *Do unto others as you would that they should do unto you* is by no means a golden rule, but the best of current silver. An honest man would have but little occasion for it. It is golden not to have any rule at all in such a case.

A Week, "Sunday"

The conscience really does not, and ought not to monopolize the whole of our lives, any more than the heart or the head. It is as liable to disease as any other part.

A Week, "Sunday"

Truth

. . . what am I to the truth I feebly utter!

Correspondence, To Calvin Greene,
February 10, 1856

No face which we can give to a matter will stead us so well at last as the truth. This alone wears well. For the most part, we are not where we are, but in a false position. . . . Say what you have to say, not what you ought. Any truth is better than make-believe.

Walden, "Conclusion"

. . . the one great rule of compassion—and if I were a professor of rhetoric I should insist on this—is, to *speak the truth.*

Miscellanies, "Last Days of John Brown"

The only way to speak the truth is to speak lovingly; only the lover's words are heard. The intellect should never speak; it is not a natural sound.

Journal, March 15, 1842

Truth never turns to rebuke falsehood; her own straightforwardness is the severest correction.

A Week, "Thursday"

I am sorry to think that you do not get a man's most effective criticism until you provoke him. Severe truth is expressed with some bitterness.

Journal, March 15, 1854

Truth is always paradoxical.

Journal, June 26, 1840

Rather than love, than money, than fame, give me truth. I sat at a table where were rich food and wine in abundance, and obsequious attendance, but sincerity and truth were not; and I went away hungry from the inhospitable board.

Walden, "Conclusion"

Sincerity

Deep are the foundations of all sincerity—even stone halls have their foundation below the frost.

Consciousness in Concord

How much sincere life before we can even utter one sincere word.

Correspondence, To Richard Fuller,
April 2, 1843

Mere innocence will tame any ferocity.

Consciousness in Concord

Perfect sincerity and transparency make a great part of beauty, as in dewdrops, lakes, and diamonds.

Journal, June 20, 1840

Philanthropy

A man is not a good *man* to me because he will feed me if I should be starving, or warm me if I should be freezing, or pull me out of a ditch if I should ever fall into one. I can find you a Newfoundland dog that will do as much. Philanthropy is not love for one's fellow-man in the broadest sense.

Walden, ''Economy''

There are a thousand hacking at the branches of evil to one who is striking at the root, and it may be that he who bestows the largest amount of time and money on the needy is doing the most by his mode of life to produce that misery which he strives in vain to relieve.

Walden, ''Economy''

Humanitarianism

It would be worth the while to ask ourselves weekly, Is our life innocent enough? Do we live *inhumanely,* toward man or beast, in thought or act? To be serene and successful we must be at one with the universe. The least conscious and needless injury inflicted on any creature is to its extent a suicide. What peace—or life—can a murderer have?

Journal, May 28, 1854

Every creature is better alive than dead, men and moose and pine trees, and he who understands it aright will rather preserve its life than destroy it.

Maine Woods, ''Chesuncook''

This haste to kill a bird or quadruped and make a skeleton of it, which many young men and some old ones exhibit, reminds me of the fable of the man who killed the hen that laid the golden eggs, and so got no more gold. It is a perfectly parallel case. Such is the knowledge which you may get from the anatomy as compared with the knowledge you get from the living creature. Every fowl lays golden eggs for him who can find them, or can detect alloy and base metal.

Journal, October 9, 1860

I have just been through the process of killing the cistudo for the sake of science; but I cannot excuse myself for this murder, and see that such actions are inconsistent with the poetic perception, however they may serve science, and will affect the quality of my observations. I pray that I may walk more innocently and serenely through nature. No reasoning whatever reconciles me to this act. It affects my day injuriously. I have lost some self-respect. I have a murderer's experience in a degree.

Journal, August 18, 1854

No humane being, past the thoughtless age of boyhood, will wantonly murder any creature which holds its life by the same tenure that he does. The hare in its extremity cries like a child. I warn you, mothers, that my sympathies do not always make the usual phil-*anthropic* distinctions.

Walden, ''Higher Laws''

I have found repeatedly, of late years, that I cannot fish without falling a little in self-respect. . . . I think that I do not mistake. It is a faint intimation, yet so are the first streaks of morning. There is unquestionably this instinct in me which belongs to the lower orders of creation; yet with every year I am less a fisherman, though without more humanity or even wisdom; at present I am no fisherman at all.

Walden, ''Higher Laws''

BIBLIOGRAPHY

Only those words used in the text are cited below. Unless otherwise noted, the following works by Thoreau belong to the "Manuscript" edition of *The Writings of Henry David Thoreau,* 20 volumes, edited by Bradford Torrey and Francis H. Allen (Boston: Houghton Mifflin & Company, 1906). Separately published essays included in the text are listed individually under the volume in which they appear in *The Writings.*

A Week on the Concord and Merrimack Rivers

Walden
   "Economy"
   "Where I Lived, and What I Lived For"
   "Reading"
   "Sounds"
   "Solitude"
   "Visitors"
   "The Village"
   "The Ponds"
   "Higher Laws"
   "Brute Neighbors"
   "House-warming"
   "Former Inhabitants; and Winter Visitors"
   "Winter Animals"
   "The Pond in Winter"
   "Spring"
   "Conclusion"

The Maine Woods
  "Ktaadn"
  "Chesuncook"
  "The Allegash and the East Branch"

Cape Cod
  "The Shipwreck"
  "The Beach Again"

Miscellanies
  "Thomas Carlyle and His Works"
  "Civil Disobedience"
  "Slavery in Massachusetts"
  "A Plea for Captain John Brown"
  "The Last Days of John Brown"
  "Life Without Principle"

A Yankee in Canada
  "Quebec and Montmorenci"

Excursions
  "Natural History of Massachusetts"
  "A Winter Walk"
  "Walking"
  "Autumnal Tints"
  "Wild Apples"
  "Night and Moonlight"

Familiar Letters and Index, ed. F. B. Sanborn

Reform Papers, ed. Wendell Glick (Princeton, New Jersey: Princeton University Press, 1973)
  "The Service"
  "Paradise (To Be) Regained"
  "Reform and Reformers"
Consciousness in Concord: The Text of Thoreau's Hitherto Lost Journal (1840-1841), notes and commentary by Perry Miller (Boston: Houghton Mifflin Co., 1958).
The Correspondence of Henry David Thoreau, eds. Walter Harding and Carl Bode (Washington Square: New York University Press, 1958).
"College Essays," in F. B. Sanborn, *The Life of Henry David Thoreau* (Boston: Houghton Mifflin Co., 1917).

SUGGESTED READING

Selected Works

Anderson, Charles, R., ed., *Thoreau's Vision: The Major Essays* (Englewood Cliffs, New Jersey: Prentice-Hall, Inc., 1973).

Bode, Carl, ed., *The Portable Thoreau* (New York: Viking Press, 1964).

Canby, Henry Seidel, ed., *The Works of Thoreau* (Boston: Houghton Mifflin Co., 1937).

Harding, Walter, annotated by, *The Variorium Walden* (New York: Twayne Publishers, Inc., 1962).

Meltzer, Milton, ed., *Thoreau: People, Principles, and Politics* (New York: Hill and Wang, 1963).

Miller, Perry, afterword by, *Walden and "Civil Disobedience"* (New York: New American Library, 1960).

Shepard, Odell, ed., *The Heart of Thoreau's Journals* (New York: Dover Publications, Inc., 1961).

Stapleton, Laurence, ed., *H. D. Thoreau: A Writer's Journal* (New York: Dover Publications, Inc., 1960).

Van Doren Stern, Philip, ed., *The Annotated Walden* (New York: Clarkson N. Potter, Inc., 1970).

Biography and Criticism

Anderson, Charles R., *The Magic Circle of Walden* (New York: Holt, Rinehart & Winston, 1968).

Andô, Shôei, *Zen and American Transcendentalism* (Tokyo: Hokuseido Press, 1970).

Canby, Henry Seidel, *Thoreau* (Boston: Houghton Mifflin Co., 1939).

Channing, William Ellery, *Thoreau: The Poet-Naturalist* (Boston: Charles E. Goodspeed, 1902).

Glick, Wendell, ed., *The Recognition of Henry David Thoreau* (Ann Arbor, Michigan: University of Michigan Press, 1969).

Harding, Walter, *The Days of Henry Thoreau* (New York: Alfred A. Knopf, Inc., 1965).

_____. ed., *The Thoreau Centennial* (New York: State University of New York Press, 1964).

_____. *A Thoreau Handbook* (New York: New York University Press, 1959).

Krutch, Joseph Wood, *Henry David Thoreau* (New York: William Sloane Associates, Inc., 1948).

Matthiessen, F. O., *American Renaissance: Art and Expression in the Age of Emerson and Whitman* (New York: Oxford University Press, 1957).

Paul, Sherman, *The Shores of America: Thoreau's Inward Exploration* (Urbana, Illinois: University of Illinois Press, 1958).

Salt, Henry S. *Life of Henry David Thoreau* (London: Walter Scott, 1836).

Sanborn, F. B., *The Life of Henry David Thoreau* (Boston: Houghton Mifflin Co., 1917).

Shanley, J. Lyndon, *The Making of Walden* (Chicago: University of Chicago Press, 1957).

Wolf, William J., *Thoreau: Mystic, Prophet, Ecologist* (Philadelphia: United Church Press, 1974).